GRADE LEVEL

K-12

A HANDBOOK FOR TEACHERS

Effective Instructional Strategies

QUADRANT D MOMENTS

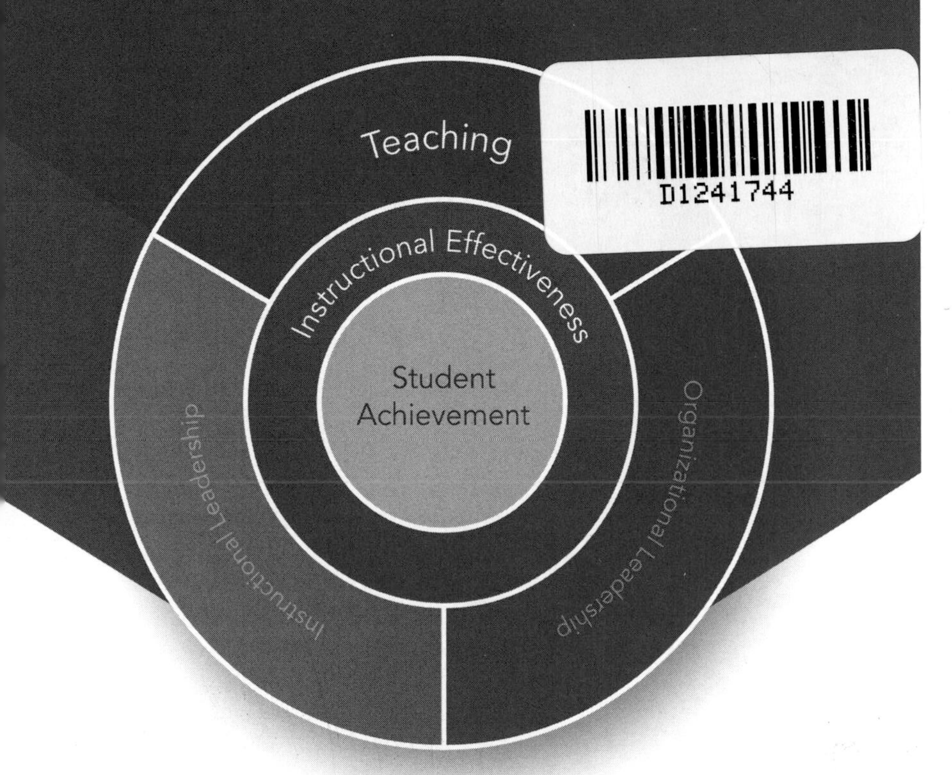

Rigor, Relevance, and Relationships for ALL Students

Acknowledgments

The International Center for Leadership in Education wishes to thank
the author of this handbook,
Richard D. Jones, Ph.D.,
and contributing author, Kathleen Weigel, Ed.D.

Published by International Center for
Leadership in Education, Inc.

Printed in the U.S.A.

ISBN-13: 978-1-935300-80-9
ISBN-10: 1-935300-80-6

International Center for Leadership in Education, Inc.
1587 Route 146
Rexford, New York 12148
(518) 399-2776
info@LeaderEd.com

010515

Contents

Overview

The Daggett System for Effective Instruction

The Daggett System for Effective Instruction (DSEI) provides a coherent focus across the entire education organization on the development and support of instructional effectiveness to improve student achievement. Whereas traditional teaching frameworks are teacher-focused and consider what teachers should do to deliver instruction, DSEI is student-focused and considers what the entire educational system should do to facilitate learning. It is a subtle but important difference based on current research and understanding about teaching and learning.

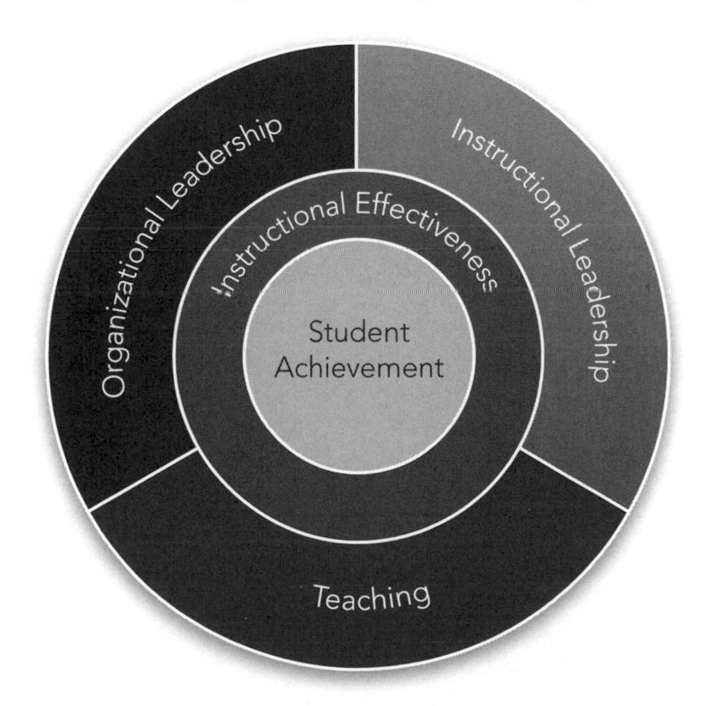

The three parts of DSEI are illustrated here. The following are the critical functions of each part of the system. Think about where you, as a professional educator, fit into this system.

Six Elements of Organizational Leadership

- Create a culture of high expectations.
- Create a shared vision.
- Build leadership capacity.
- Align organizational structures and systems to vision.
- Align teacher/administrator selection, support, and evaluation.
- Support decision making with data systems.

Five Elements of Instructional Leadership

- Use research to establish urgency for higher expectations.
- Align curriculum to standards.
- Integrate literacy and math across all content areas.
- Facilitate data-driven decision making to inform instruction.
- Provide opportunities for focused professional collaboration and growth.

Six Elements of Teaching

- Embrace rigorous and relevant expectations for all students.
- Build strong relationships with students.
- Possess depth of content knowledge and make it relevant to students.
- Facilitate rigorous and relevant instruction based on how students learn.
- Demonstrate expertise in use of instructional strategies, technology, and best practices.
- Use assessments to guide and differentiate instruction.

When all parts of the system are working together efficiently, teachers receive the support they need, and students are successfully prepared for college, careers, and citizenship.

Effective Instructional Strategies—Quadrant D Moments

Based on the Rigor/Relevance Framework, this handbook presents 20 short strategies that will enable a teacher to introduce Quadrant D Moments into every class period to raise the level of rigor and relevance.

The Rigor/Relevance Framework is based on two dimensions of higher standards and student achievement. Quadrant D indicates an activity that maximizes both measurements. The strategies presented here were designed to provide learning opportunities for different learning styles and multiple intelligences. The handbook explains ways in which the strategies can be adapted to various subjects and different grade levels.

Around You

This strategy assists students in building the relevance of a curriculum as it relates to themselves, their local community, work, or other real-world materials.

At Your Service

This D-moment strategy links classroom learning to opportunities outside the classroom. Students identify or perform a simple act or service that would benefit individuals, the school, or the neighborhood.

Can You See It Now?

Teachers can use this strategy to shift learning from a verbal/linguistic experience to a more visual or tactile experience. Students are asked to translate numbers or concepts into visible, tangible objects in order to visualize and more deeply understand complex ideas.

Current Events

Teachers can use this strategy to help students connect any content to real-world current events.

Fix It

This strategy challenges students to rework a solution to a problem that the student has already attempted but has answered incorrectly. The strategy leads students to identify and correct the mistake, omission, or error in logic.

Future Think

This strategy asks students to predict the future based on current scientific or historical knowledge.

Google It

Teachers will use this strategy to extend teachable moments by asking students to use Internet search engines to answer questions.

How Did That Happen?

This D-moment strategy builds on students' natural curiosity. Students use cause and effect analysis to determine why a real-life phenomenon, event, or action occurred.

In Your Own Words

Students summarize key points from reading, viewing, or presentations and relate them to their lives or future.

Justify Your Position

With this strategy, students take a position on a real-world issue that impacts someone and develop a rational to defend it with a logical argument and citation of facts.

Learning with Peers

This strategy enables students to learn from and with each other by sharing prior knowledge, ideas, and experiences. Students work in pairs or small groups. The strategy is effective for reteaching or reinforcing learning.

LegoLand

Students create or manipulate objects to represent a concept in a lesson. It can be used with Legos or any form of hands-on manipulatives. The strategy stimulates creativity and thinking by involving touch and connection between the fingers and the brain.

Media Circus

Students relate television shows, movies, music, or other media to concepts learned in class.

Original Answers

Original Answers emphasizes the process of learning rather than the acquisition of knowledge. Students arrive at a unique answer to an open-ended problem or create an original way to display knowledge or data.

QuickWrites

This strategy asks students to write in short bursts (1-5 minutes) to pose questions, reflect, discover answers, check for understanding, and stimulate discussion.

Quiz Show

This D-moment strategy challenges students to craft clear and precise questions to elicit reasonable answers for a student quiz show.

Remind Me

This strategy challenges students to develop a real-world metaphor for complex content to help them remember relationships, rules, patterns, or content.

Tell Me a Story

Students create fanciful stories about real or fictional events as a means to share knowledge, remember ideas, or explain concepts.

What If?

Students analyze a current condition and imagine the impact of change. It might be used with historical events or variables in a mathematical operation, for example.

"Why" Questions

Students pose "why" questions on content for inquiry, exploring additional learning, or reflection on why learning is important to their lives or future.

Introduction

Effective Instructional Strategies – Quadrant D Moments is another in the International Center for Leadership in Education's series of publications on teaching for rigor and relevance. These resources are based on the Rigor/Relevance Framework, a tool developed by the International Center to measure the rigor and relevance of curriculum, instruction, and assessment. Once teachers are familiar with the Framework, they can use it to facilitate learning experiences for students that are high in cognitive skill development and that relate to real-world situations.

In 2001 Bloom's Knowledge Taxonomy was updated and revised by Lorin Anderson, a student of Bloom's, and David Krathwohl, a colleague, to reflect the movement to standards-based curricula and assessment. Nouns in Bloom's original model were changed to verb forms (for example, *knowledge* to *remembering* and *comprehension* to *understanding*) and slightly reordered. We believe that the original Bloom's taxonomy as shown in our Rigor/Relevance Framework clearly describes expectations for Quadrants A, B, C, and D. The revised Bloom's elevates the importance of Quadrants B and D and indicates how 21st-century lessons should be built. We regard both the original and revised taxonomies as necessary and important.

A frequent misconception about teaching for high rigor and high relevance is that it requires complex projects and problem-based learning that take significant amounts of instructional time. While those "big" projects are effective learning activities, teachers can also use short teaching strategies within a single class period to raise the level of rigor and/or relevance. Quadrant D Moments give teachers ways they can extend student learning into Quadrant D every day, using these brief instructional strategies that raise the level of rigor and relevance.

Using the Rigor/Relevance Framework®

The Rigor/Relevance Framework is based on the two dimensions of higher standards and student achievement.

First, a continuum of knowledge describes the increasingly complex ways in which we think. This Knowledge Taxonomy is based on the six levels of the well-known Bloom's Taxonomy: (1) knowledge/awareness, (2) comprehension, (3) application, (4) analysis, (5) synthesis, and (6) evaluation.

The low end of this continuum involves acquiring knowledge and being able to recall or locate that knowledge in a simple manner. Just as a computer completes a word search in a word processing program, a competent person at this level can scan thousands of bits of information in the brain to locate that desired knowledge. The recall of knowledge can be easy or hard. It is easy when the information is common knowledge (held by many). Recall of knowledge is hard when it is information known only to a few.

The high end of the Knowledge Taxonomy labels more complex ways in which individuals use knowledge. At this level, knowledge is fully integrated into one's mind, and individuals can do much more than locate information — they can take several pieces of knowledge and combine them in both logical and creative ways. Assimilation of knowledge is a good way to describe this high level of the thinking continuum. Assimilation is often referred to as a higher order thinking skill; at this level, the student can solve multistep problems, create unique work, and devise solutions.

The second continuum, created by Willard Daggett, is known as the Application Model. The five levels of this continuum are: (1) knowledge in one discipline, (2) apply in discipline, (3) apply across disciplines, (4) apply to real-world predictable situations, and (5) apply to real-world unpredictable situations. The Application Model describes putting knowledge to use: The low end is knowledge acquired for its own sake; the high end signifies action — use of that knowledge to solve complex real-world problems and to create projects, designs, and other works for use in real-world situations.

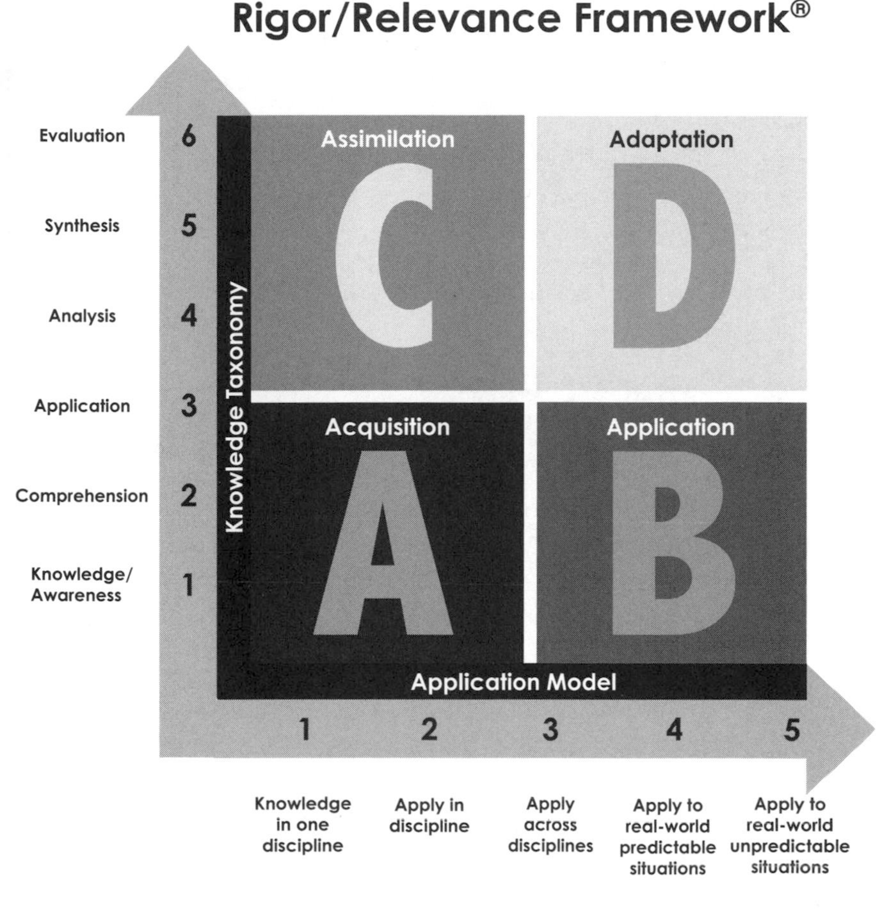

The Rigor/Relevance Framework has four quadrants.

Quadrant A represents simple recall and basic understanding of knowledge for its own sake. Quadrant C represents more complex thinking, but still knowledge for its own sake.

Quadrant A acknowledges easy recall of information, such as knowing that the world is round and that Shakespeare wrote *Hamlet*.

Quadrant C embraces higher levels of knowledge, such as knowing complex math and science, analyzing literature, and examining the benefits and challenges of the cultural diversity of the United States versus other nations.

Quadrants B and D are based on action or high degrees of application. Quadrant B would include knowing how to use math skills to make purchases and count change, or how to perform physical tasks in art or music. The ability to apply knowledge from a variety of sources to solve complex problems or to create real-world products are types of Quadrant D learning.

One way to think about the Rigor/Relevance Framework in day-to-day instruction is in terms of the roles that teachers and students take. These roles are represented in the following figure. When instruction and expected student learning is in Quadrant A, the focus is on "teacher work." Teachers expend energy to create and assess learning activities – providing information, creating worksheets, and grading student work. The student is often a passive learner.

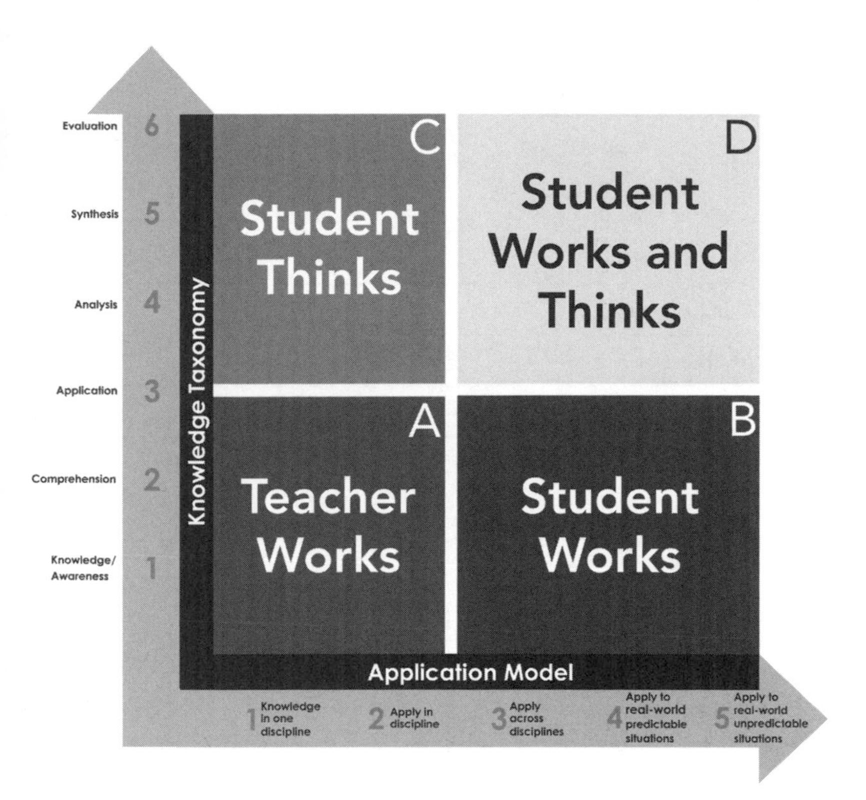

Learning Styles and Multiple Intelligences

Every student learns differently. If teachers are to be effective facilitators of every student reaching a level of proficiency, they need to incorporate a variety of strategies. By using a variety of strategies, teachers create more interesting and engaging instruction that is more likely to enable each student to learn. In this discussion of D-moment teaching strategies, it is appropriate to analyze each of these strategies in terms of its relationship to learning styles and multiple intelligences. Learning styles are divided into two categories. The first category is Sensory Mode, which distinguishes students' preferences for the senses they are most comfortable in using to acquire new learning. The common categories of Sensory Modes of learning styles are visual, auditory, tactile, and kinesthetic. Table 1 shows the relationship of each of these D-moment strategies to these four sensory modes.

Table 1. Quadrant D Moments and Sensory Modes of Learning Styles

	Visual	Auditory	Tactual	Kinesthetic
Around You	✓			
At Your Service			✓	✓
Can You See It Now?	✓		✓	✓
Current Events		✓		
Fix It	✓			
Future Think	✓			
Google It	✓		✓	
How Did That Happen?		✓		
In Your Own Words		✓		
Justify Your Position		✓		
Learning with Peers		✓		
LegoLand			✓	✓
Media Circus	✓	✓		
Original Answers	✓	✓		
QuickWrites	✓		✓	
Quiz Show	✓	✓		
Remind Me	✓			
Tell Me a Story		✓		
What If?		✓		
"Why" Questions		✓		

A second aspect of learning styles is students' preferred Thinking Mode when processing the new learning. Two common dimensions of thinking, as defined by Anthony Gregorc, are whether students rely on more concrete thinking or more abstract thinking and whether they are more sequential in thinking or more random. Four broad categories of thinking styles, based on these two variables, are listed below (Gregorc, A. *The Mind Styles™ Model: Theory, Principles, and Applications.* Columbia, CT: Gregorc Associates, 1984.):

- **Concrete-Sequential** learners are well organized, enjoy recalling and constructing correct responses, and are consistent and focused in learning.
- **Abstract-Sequential** learners are analytical thinkers, follow traditional instruction, and are comfortable working alone and giving long answers.
- **Concrete-Random** learners respond to opportunities to be creative and design products, are usually self-directed, and like to experiment.
- **Abstract-Random** learners respond to creative learning activities, prefer working with others in a collaborative environment, and are frequently difficult to keep on task.

Table 2 shows each of the D-moment strategies in relation to these thinking preferences of learning styles.

Table 2. Quadrant D Moments and Thinking Modes of Learning Styles

	Concrete-Sequential	Concrete-Random	Abstract-Sequential	Abstract-Random
Around You		✓		✓
At Your Service		✓		✓
Can You See It Now?		✓		
Current Events	✓			✓
Fix It	✓	✓	✓	
Future Think		✓		✓
Google It	✓			
How Did That Happen?	✓		✓	✓
In Your Own Words	✓		✓	
Justify Your Position	✓		✓	
Learning with Peers				✓
LegoLand		✓		✓
Media Circus		✓		✓
Original Answers	✓	✓		
QuickWrites	✓		✓	
Quiz Show		✓		✓
Remind Me			✓	✓
Tell Me a Story		✓		✓
What If?			✓	✓
"Why" Questions	✓		✓	

Howard Gardner's multiple-intelligence theory has become a standard model, used to understand many aspects of human intelligence and teach appropriately to them. Gardner lists nine intelligences. Intelligences are not the same as learning styles, although there are some similarities in terms. Learning styles relate to the preferences that individuals have in taking in and processing new knowledge and skills. Multiple intelligences are the innate gifts that some individuals have for learning different knowledge and skills. These intelligences explain how individuals show strong interests and increased abilities to learn certain skills and knowledge. Many psychologists debate the physiological existence of different intelligences. However, educators know from experience that students demonstrate these different intelligences on a daily basis.

The nine intelligences are (Gardner, H. *Intelligence Reframed: Multiple Intelligences for the 21st Century*. New York: Basic Books, 1999.):

- **Verbal/Linguistic** — naturally good with writing or speaking and memorization
- **Logical/Mathematical** — driven by logic and reasoning
- **Visual/Spatial** — good at remembering images and aware of surroundings
- **Bodily/Kinesthetic** — love movement, have good motor skills, and are aware of their bodies
- **Musical** — musically gifted, with a "good ear" for rhythm and composition
- **Intrapersonal** — adept at looking inward
- **Interpersonal** — good with people and able to thrive in social interactions
- **Naturalist** — have a sensitivity to and appreciation for nature
- **Existential** — like to ponder, question, and think about "big picture" and mysteries of life

Awareness of these intelligences and relating these to the D-moment strategies can help teachers recognize how students will respond to and engage in these strategies and which students will need more time or assistance to learn. (See Table 3.)

Table 3. Quadrant D Moments and Multiple Intelligences

	Verbal/Linguistic	Logical/ Mathematical	Visual/Spatial	Bodily/Kinesthetic	Musical	Intrapersonal	Interpersonal	Naturalist	Existential
Around You		✓	✓			✓	✓	✓	✓
At Your Service						✓	✓	✓	
Can You See it Now?		✓	✓	✓					
Current Events	✓		✓					✓	
Fix It		✓							
Future Think	✓						✓		✓
Google It	✓	✓							
How Did That Happen?		✓	✓						✓
In Your Own Words	✓						✓		✓
Justify Your Position	✓	✓							
Learning With Peers						✓	✓		
LegoLand			✓	✓					
Media Circus			✓		✓		✓		
Original Answers	✓						✓		
QuickWrites	✓								
Quiz Show		✓							
Remind Me	✓	✓							
Tell Me A Story	✓		✓				✓		
What If?		✓							✓
"Why" Questions	✓	✓							✓

Descriptions of D-Moments

Each Quadrant D Moment is described in the following chapters under these headings:

Overview

This gives a general description of the instructional strategy and some general ways to use it in the classroom.

Pedagogy Perspective

The information in the tables just presented is repeated to show the relationship of that D-moment to learning styles and multiple intelligences.

What Makes It High Rigor/Relevance?

This section explains the rationale and the characteristics of this strategy that make it high rigor and high relevance.

How to Use It

Tips for using the strategy are offered to stimulate thinking and ideas for incorporating D-moments into daily instruction.

Where to Use It

The final section presents a number of specific instructional examples for using this strategy in various subjects in grades pre-K–5 and grades 6–12. Many of the activities can be adapted to students of different ages and to different content areas. Teachers can use their creativity to adapt these D-moment activities to teach for high rigor and high relevance every day.

Around You

Overview

Around You is a D-moment in which the content that students are studying is connected to the students' world. This connection could occur as students personally reflect on their own characteristics and traits. It could be a connection to students' family, to their cultural heritage, or to their community/neighborhood.

Around You is primarily about building relevance — where students see the curriculum as it relates to their individual lives. In mathematics, this might be where students are asked to use data about themselves or data that they collect in performing mathematical operations. Another area of mathematics might be observing geometry in the natural and human-made world. In science, instruction might be extended to relate science inquiry to individual student lives, as students observe phenomena in their community and pose questions to understand it. In English language arts, teachers could ask students to make connections between the literature they are reading and their individual lives. In writing, students build a strong rigor and relevance experience any time the writing assignment is about reflecting on themselves, their lives, and their experiences.

Pedagogy Perspective

Around You is an ideal strategy for students with the following learning styles and intelligences.

Sensory Mode	Visual
Thinking Modes	Concrete-Random Abstract-Random
Multiple Intelligences	Logical/Mathematical Visual/Spatial Interpersonal Intrapersonal Naturalist Existential

What Makes It High Rigor/Relevance?

This D-moment is particularly high in rigor and relevance because students are connecting the curriculum to personal experiences. This adds relevance to instruction and student application of skills and knowledge to their own experiences.

Using the ***Around You*** D-moment, students are challenged to think analytically to make the connection within the curriculum. They are not asked to learn separate facts and isolated skills, but rather to observe and understand how the skills and knowledge directly relate to their individual lives. This requires a higher level of thinking and moves into high relevance.

How to Use It

Around You can be used at the beginning of the lesson, when introducing new information. This creates an environment that is more interesting to students, helping them see the connection between the upcoming lesson and their particular lives. An ***Around You*** D-moment can be an emotional hook to engage students in the lesson. Students are more often emotionally charged and excited when they are part of the discussion and are reflecting on their individual lives. Emotions are critical to engaging students in learning, and an activity that connects them to the learning can be a way to increase motivation and heighten emotional interest.

Around You can also be a higher-level thinking skill by initiating a compare-and-contrast that extends students' observations of the real world. It is important to make frequent comparisons between new content and individual lives and also to showcase the contrasting differences. This could include comparing differences in cultures studied or historical periods to students' current lives.

One important aspect of teaching ***Around You*** is taking a balanced and culturally relevant approach so that every student feels a part of the class.

- Avoid calling on individual students; when necessary, call on each student equitably.
- Ensure that lessons include role models from the cultural groups represented in your classroom.
- Get to know students' interests; this provides ideas for connecting their lives to the curriculum.
- Use student names in examples.
- Use cooperative learning and group work frequently.
- Emphasize cooperation and deemphasize competition.
- Use a "We're all in this together" classroom approach.
- Build a classroom community that expects excellence from each student and allows a flexible time frame for achieving excellence.
- Talk explicitly about the negative effects of peer pressure and how students can counteract them.
- Ask students to bring in a family item and share it with the class.
- Invite parents into the school to interact with staff and students.
- Begin the year by having students write personal narratives about themselves.

- If teaching a subject other than English language arts, tie the assignment to that subject matter and classroom goals. Ask students to write their "math history" or their "science history" (or other subject) and tell how that subject has been a part of their lives. Have them end their history with their goals for the class.

Where to Use It

Following are examples of using this D-moment in different subjects and at different grade levels.

All Grades

- **Current social issue.** After reading a poem that relates to a current social issue, have students connect the issues indicated in the poem with the current social issue.
- **World languages.** When studying holidays of different cultures, ask students to compare and contrast those holidays with national holidays in the United States.

Grades Pre-K–5

- **Relate text to experiences.** Develop a standard routine for asking students to relate a particular text to other experiences in their prior knowledge. Start with text to text, where students relate what they are reading to another text they have read. Move on to text to self, where students relate the text to themselves and their lives. Conclude with text to world, where students consider how the text relates to the world today.
- **Retell a story.** Have students retell a story that they have listened to, using themselves as the main character.
- **Compare and contrast rules.** When working with students to understand school and classroom rules, have students compare and contrast these rules with community laws and social manners.

Grades 6–12

- **Character education.** Each day, introduce a character-education topic and discuss examples of real-life situations in which character, honesty, courage, integrity, respect, attitude, compassion, and so on are important. Then assign students a character-education life topic that they will introduce and teach to their classmates. They will be challenged to encourage the class to think critically and to change their lives for the better as a result of hearing classmates' presentations on positive characteristics.
- **World languages.** When students are studying world languages, point out cultural differences by taking an authentic advertisement, map, or travel brochure from the host country and having students translate the material. After students have made a literal translation, have them analyze the cultural differences and suggest modifications to use this same advertisement or promotion in their community.
- **Genetic traits.** When studying biology, have students generate a family tree. Using the tree, they trace the inheritance of genetic traits. Encourage students to trace diseases such as diabetes, heart disease, and so on. Then discuss the possible ramifications of students' "genetic geneology" when they decide to have children.
- **Mythology skits.** While studying Greek mythology, have students create short skits to demonstrate how a chosen mythological character would solve a typical high school problem, such as missing the school bus, not making a team, or being bullied.
- **Real-world mathematics.** When studying mathematical calculations and equations with multiple unknowns, give students a real-world problem that relates to objects in and around the school. For example, take different-sized boxes from the school cafeteria and determine which could be used most cost effectively to sell and transport other products.
- **Area of irregular shapes.** After reviewing circles, rectangles, trapezoids, and triangles, have students arrive at solutions for resurfacing a pool deck. Give students shapes around the pool that need to be resurfaced and prices per square foot of different materials. Then give students fictitious quotes and ask if those quotes are reasonable for the cost of resurfacing.

At Your Service

Overview

At Your Service is a D-moment in which students connect classroom content and instructional strategies to meaningful service activities that promote acquisition of skills and knowledge. ***At Your Service*** is a form of service learning that increases relevance by linking classroom learning to opportunities outside the classroom. It is the purest form of a Quadrant D activity, as acquired knowledge from the classroom is tested, implemented, and executed in a real-world setting. Willard Wirtz, former Secretary of Labor, was quoted as saying, "There aren't two worlds — education and work; there is one world — life." School is the training ground for the world of work. Classroom knowledge should enable students to apply academic principles to practical, everyday problems. When students become immersed in neighborhood, community, and school activities, they are able to participate and contribute for the greater good. Doing so allows them to practice and cultivate their individual leadership abilities and skills. ***At Your Service*** provides the training ground to assist students as they enter adulthood. Students are expected to create, participate, and implement programs that are mutually beneficial and that contribute to successful outcomes and meaningful community interaction. The end result is one that is valued by those being served.

Pedagogy Perspective

At Your Service is an ideal strategy for students with the following learning styles and intelligences.

Sensory Modes	Tactile Kinesthetic
Thinking Modes	Concrete-Random Abstract-Random
Multiple Intelligences	Interpersonal Intrapersonal Naturalistic

What Makes It High Rigor/Relevance?

This D-moment has high rigor and relevance because of its strong real-world connection. In this D-moment, students are connecting classroom experiences and prior knowledge to real-world activities. They are able to identify an issue and perform a service that benefits individuals, schools, or neighborhoods. This makes the curriculum rich and relevant with the real-world application; it requires skills, prior knowledge, and deductive and inductive reasoning to either fix the problem or contribute to some societal issue.

When using the ***At Your Service*** D-moment, students are required to dig deeply into their memories, transfer knowledge and skills, develop interpersonal skills, analyze situations, solve problems, and make decisions. Students then use this knowledge to think about complex community problems and alternate solutions. This D-moment not only develops the social, personal side of the student but also links curriculum to meaningful service and civic responsibility.

How to Use It

The *At Your Service* D-moment can be used at the beginning of the lesson to pose a problem for which students find an appropriate solution. It can also be used at the end of a concept as a final project to determine mastery of the content. Student engagement should be extraordinarily high: Not only are the activities intellectually charged, but they also involve the students physically. Higher-level thinking skills are required for students to apply this D-moment to real-world issues. By making comparative analysis to situations within the community, students may see how daily subject matter applies to the real world.

An important aspect of teaching *At Your Service* is ensuring that relevant issues are being represented in a balanced format. Emphasis should be placed on meaningful service and positive community outcome.

- Determine a genuine need.
- Analyze potential partnerships, anticipated resources needed, relationship with existing curriculum, appropriate supervision for students, and appropriate developmental levels for all student participation and learning outcomes.
- Ensure that students work in teams, each student having an equal part.
- Explore all issues within a specific setting to determine the best course of action.
- Provide a variety of current issues for investigation.
- Afford students the opportunity to analyze all facets of the specific project.
- Emphasize cooperation and group work.
- Establish a specific plan of action, with students determining all elements.
- Determine the desired outcome.
- Invite stakeholders to participate and interact with students and staff.
- Create a celebration for success.

The beauty of ***At Your Service*** is that it provides an opportunity for students to participate in a variety of interdisciplinary, cross-curricular units. No matter what the grade level, any aspect could be developed, designed, and executed through all subject areas. Doing so would provide for a much richer experience.

Where to Use It

Following are examples of using this D-moment in different subjects and at different grade levels.

All Grades

- **English language arts.** After reading stories concerning social ills, have students identify current problems relating to those same issues. Students could be divided into groups to discuss the current related issues and create a project to benefit a school or community issue.
- **Create a garden.** Have students determine the process for growing plants and the use of photosynthesis. They can create a garden to grow vegetables and fruits. The proceeds could be donated to a local soup kitchen to feed the hungry.
- **Social studies.** Have students pair with an English language arts class that is studying community needs and participate in a collaborative project to support the ideas in the language arts class.
- **Practical mathematics.** Have students participate in a science project about growing food by measuring plots of land and determining the amounts of water and soil and the location of plants. All mathematical computations relating to the project would come from this class.
- **Serve seniors.** Encourage students to visit the local senior center and help seniors decorate for a holiday.

Grades Pre-K–5

- **Character development.** When teaching young students about character development, introduce keywords to live by, such as *responsibility, respect, honesty, pride,* and *fairness*. Each month, highlight a keyword and ask students to write a personal goal that identifies a simple act of service. This will emphasize and exemplify that keyword. At the end of the month, ask students to write a journal entry, explaining how they met their goal for performing that keyword in some sort of service to someone else.

- **Food for the needy.** Have students discuss resources needed to live, including food. Ask students to suggest ways to help others in need of food and then design and plan the collection of nonperishable foods. Students could set up a food shelter at the school and collect items to give those in need. As part of this activity, students will sort and organize the food pantry and then determine the appropriate means for distribution of the food to those in need.
- **Community performance.** Visit a senior citizen facility and have students create and play a game with the adults. Students could also learn songs, skits, and activities to share with the adults.
- **Student issues.** When reading a theme about friendship and helping others, discussions can lead to problems in the neighborhood such as safety, lighting, and fast automobiles. Brainstorm with students about what bothers them the most. Then locate the addresses of officials who handle those issues within the community and have students prepare to contact them. Emphasize to students the importance of persuasive conversation and writing when dealing with important issues. Perhaps even have students invite the officials to come to the school and interact with the class personally.
- **Measurement and recycling.** Ask students to collect something simple, like pennies or bottles to be recycled. Have them determine how much money has been collected. Place students in small groups and have them debate the issue of the appropriate use for the funds that they have raised. Build consensus to determine the appropriate use and donate the funds accordingly, having representative students present the money.
- **Helping others.** Students could read a story with the theme of doing something good for others. Have students brainstorm what they might do to help someone with a similar need in their school or community.

Grades 6–12

- **Neighborhood cleanup.** Ask students to discuss various ways to keep their school and neighborhood clean. In small groups, jigsaw an activity for the students to execute each facet of the campus or neighborhood cleanup. Individual groups could work on timeline, resources needed, personnel, supervision, and any other facet necessary to complete the project.
- **Character development.** When introducing a character lesson on service to the community, have students read a story related to service. Have students brainstorm their own list of how to help others in school and at home. Then ask students to choose the one service they feel is most important and write about how that particular service is an act of kindness. Invite students to sign a pledge about providing service to others. They may also wish to have a specific day called "A Random Act of Kindness" and spend that day doing nice things for others.
- **Graph for fundraising.** Students often question why they are not allowed to wear hats in school. Plan a day on which students can pay one dollar to wear their hat. All funds can then be presented to a local hospital for children with cancer. Have students graph the amount of money collected in each class to determine which class contributed the most.
- **Reflect and write.** Have students collect food and donate it to a local soup kitchen or food bank, delivering the food and talking to people receiving the food. Then ask students to reflect on the experience of meeting people in need by discussing or writing in a reflective way in class the next day. Students will see how rewarding it is to help others.
- **Clubs and community.** Encourage groups of students from clubs and organizations to participate in a community event called "Paint Up Your Town." Under the supervision of teachers and community members, students help paint and clean the homes of the elderly within their own community. The interaction, impact, and results would be everlasting.
- **Apply reading.** After introducing reading strategies, have students describe a situation to which they can apply ***At Your Service*** to understand a particular story or piece of text.

- **Acts of compassion.** When reading a novel or piece of fiction in which the main character learns the concept of compassion, extend this service learning by having students share observations of acts of compassion. Then plan a service project.
- **Technology.** When discussing the changing technology, have students research the options for recycling old technology. Perhaps create a digital divide project, in which recycled technology (computers and the like) is refurbished and redistributed to the needy of the community.

Can You See It Now?

Overview

Can You See It Now? is a D-moment strategy in which teachers create visual or movement activities to illustrate complex learning concepts. The name ***Can You See It Now?*** implies making the learning more visible to the student, but it can also include activities that help to trigger deeper student understanding. ***Can You See It Now?*** is a particularly effective strategy to shift a learning experience from a routine verbal/linguistic learning experience to one that is more visual and/or tactile.

A teacher might have students act out a scene from a book they are reading, illustrate a math concept with manipulatives, or represent a microscopic cell structure with large objects in the classroom. As students are developing their learning skills, one of the most challenging aspects for them is to understand things that they cannot see or that have not been part of their personal experience. By using this D-moment strategy, teachers can help to bridge the gap between important concepts and knowledge within the curriculum and students' daily experiences.

Pedagogy Perspective

Can You See It Now? is an ideal strategy for students with the following learning styles and intelligences.

Sensory Modes	Visual Tactile Kinesthetic
Thinking Modes	Concrete-Random Abstract-Random
Multiple Intelligences	Logical/Mathematical Visual/Spatial Bodily/Kinesthetic

What Makes It High Rigor/Relevance?

This particular D-moment strategy is useful in increasing relevance within the curriculum. By using ***Can You See It Now?*** teachers are actually bridging the gap between more abstract learning and the real-world experiences of the student. Consequently, these instructional activities are very high on the Application Model of the Rigor/Relevance Framework. ***Can You See It Now?*** also increases student thinking because it requires students to analyze information. Students come to realize that there are multiple ways to represent knowledge. Knowledge can be represented in a literary form with typical language, or it can be in a more visual form. By using more visual strategies, students understand the connections between different representations of knowledge and increase their level of thinking as a result of those experiences.

The ***Can You See It Now?*** D-moment increases the relevance of student learning and, in the process, moves students' thinking toward higher levels of rigor.

How to Use It

When introducing new information to students, pay attention to body language that may indicate a lack of understanding. This will be a good time to explore an alternate way of introducing information, perhaps in a more visual form or some other form that will help their understanding. By frequently checking for understanding, you can flag those times when an alternate strategy, such as this D-moment, is needed. To use this D-moment effectively, look to add relevance by reframing the information in the experiences that a student already has or by using visual depictions that can be created within the classroom.

One of the important aspects of making the learning more visual is to use common strategies that help to promote a nonverbal/visual learning style:

- Make extensive use of pictures, graphics, and other visuals in the classroom.
- Incorporate videos and slides when making presentations.
- Use graphic organizers to capture, store, and reuse information.
- Organize information in graphs and flow charts to represent data.
- Encourage students to take the time to highlight key points or vocabulary words in their reading.
- Have students create visual cues or prompts to aid in remembering important information.

Taking the time to introduce learning experiences that cater to visual learners will often help every student understand the key information in the lesson. It not only helps to ensure that a lesson reaches students with multiple learning styles, it also reinforces to students that there are multiple ways to learn. It is also a good opportunity to check students' understanding. When students observe or participate in a ***Can You See It Now?*** D-moment, teachers often notice a change in body language that indicates a greater understanding of the learning.

Where to Use It

Following are some examples of using this D-moment in different subjects and at different grade levels.

All Grades

- **Scale drawings.** Have students make scale and actual drawings of objects such as the Statue of Liberty and mark the dimensions by using masking tape on the floor of the classroom or playground to give a better concept of size and proportion.

Grades Pre-K–5

- **Earth science and writing**. Connect the two subjects by using yarn to construct lines of latitude and longitude across the ceiling. Define the equator and place coordinates for each line. Have students place their published writing papers on a coordinate and then write directions to their paper on an index card, using coordinate and cardinal numbers. During the celebration to showcase their work, distribute cards randomly to groups of students. Have a group start at the equator and find the way to the published piece by following the directions. Follow the same procedure with other groups to evaluate whether or not directions were written correctly.
- **Holidays.** Apply student learning at holidays. In December, have students make picture frames to give to parents as presents. Have students measure the length of the ribbon used to decorate the frame by first calculating the perimeter of the frame. Around Thanksgiving, ask students to plan a Thanksgiving dinner, given a budget, and to cut out pictures with the prices of items from supermarket flyers.
- **Geography.** Use opportunities to connect geography and stories. For example, when reading about immigration, students can share examples from their own family's immigration to the United States or migration within the United States. Use an atlas to identify where these countries and states are located.

- **Recycling/measuring garbage.** Have students read, research, and write articles on recycling around the home. Also read them the book *Just a Dream* by Chris Van Allsburg, which may inspire them to measure their trash. For example, have students put into a bag all the garbage they create in one day. At the end of the day, have them sort the garbage and do a math test, estimating the amounts of garbage each student produced. Encourage students to think about what the world would be like without recycling.
- **Measurement.** Give students various measuring containers in metric and English measures. Have them fill these containers with water and measure amounts of water to show relationships between these quantities and then create a graphic to represent the relationship of different volume measures.
- **Poetry.** When they are writing poetry, allow students to make visual representations (using clay, paint, and so on) to go with their writing or to use a picture or object from their lives as an inspiration.
- **Mathematics.** When teaching students to do basic computation, have students do calculations about familiar transactions. For example, you could ask, "How much money would you spend if you bought the school lunch every day for the whole school year?"
- **How big?** In reading, when encountering a reference to the size of a particular object (such as a canoe from early Native Americans), take a moment to have students actually calculate the height and physically represent the size in the classroom so that they can better appreciate the size.
- **Physical and chemical changes.** As a review of physical and chemical changes, have students construct the outline for a game called "From the Cafeteria to the Restroom." Students work together to identify all the physical and chemical changes that occurred in the cafeteria, from the preparation of their food to when the food was digested and excreted. Students reflect on their own experiences and evaluate their surroundings through the lens of these changes.

- **Natural disasters.** When reading about natural disasters, have students locate these disasters on a map and research the number of people affected by the disaster in each region.
- **Spelling.** Give large block letters to two teams of students. When reviewing spelling words, have each team assemble the correct spelling of the word, with students moving into position with their block letters. Make it a competition to see which team spells the word correctly first.
- **Build it.** After studying Native American cultures, have students use index cards to construct a tepee, which they can decorate with symbols of the Plains Indian culture.
- **Skip counting.** When introducing this concept, have students use actual coins of different values to do the counting.
- **Animal study.** When studying animals, take the class outside and unroll a piece of yarn as long as a blue whale (about 100 feet) to demonstrate the animal's immense size.
- **Physical education.** Ask students to figure out how many students on a team are necessary to make the game successful. They need to figure the number of teams and the number of students on a team necessary to play the game.

Grades 6–12

- **Scale models.** To help students understand scale, have them create a model or scale drawing of a sporting field or court. They must state the scale used and explain how they converted the dimensions for the model or drawing. As students present models or drawings to the class, have them explain the process used and how they completed the task.
- **Graphical presentations.** Have students use recent newspapers from consecutive days to find data to analyze and compare. Students take data that is hard to understand (not in graphical form) and put it into graphical presentations (such as a whisker plot) to make it easier to understand.
- **Lawmaking process.** Have students bring in an article about a current issue, such as healthcare. On a bulletin board, use mapping to show the path that a bill must take before it can be put

into law. Over time, track the progress of that issue toward becoming a law. Doing so will give students a visual representation of the lawmaking process.

- **Physics.** Have students calculate the density of various objects (different materials, shapes, and so on). Doing so can help students see how copper has the same density no matter the size of the piece. Also, large objects can have smaller densities and vice versa.
- **Home calculations.** Have students create a floor plan of their dream house. Calculate how much it would cost to carpet certain rooms in the house at a specific price per square foot. Also calculate the length of molding in various rooms.
- **Geometry.** Give students hollow plastic solids (rectangular prism, pyramid, cone, cylinder, sphere) and a bag of rice. Using the formula for the volume of a rectangular prism, have them derive formulas for the other solids by pouring rice and seeing the amounts that the solids hold. Students then discover the other formulas.
- **Big numbers.** Have students apply math to current events that mention large numbers. For example, refer to a statistic of one million viewers of a YouTube video and have students calculate how many hours or days of viewing time that is. Another example might be presenting data on the amount of candy sold at Halloween and having students figure out the total calories consumed.
- **Pioneers.** When studying westward expansion and the early pioneers, ask students to make a list of items they would take on a western journey. Then use chalk to measure and draw the actual size of the covered wagon on the playground and use boxes to represent the items they wanted to take. Students then revise their list to include only items that would be essential to take and that would fit in the wagon.
- **Discover formulas.** Give students 24 one-inch squares to arrange in all possible ways; then have them write out the related multiplication facts.
- **Role-play.** Have students role-play a historical event that they read about in order to capture the emotion of an event. For exam-

ple, when studying about the Revolutionary War, have students role-play the king, parliament, and tax collectors. Other students can be colonists who have small amounts of money. The king taxes colonists on arbitrary items such as who wears glasses or certain color shirts. Tax collectors collect money from that group of colonists and give it to the parliament and the king. Then have students write about the emotions they felt while being taxed.

- **Ancient Asia.** When studying ancient Asia, have students relate the dimensions of the Great Wall of China to a scale that would fit on the school grounds. Students can walk the scale version of the Great Wall and estimate the time to traverse the actual Great Wall. Have students consider alternate means of getting around on the Great Wall.

Current Events

Overview

Today, there is a wealth of information available about current events. Twenty-four-hour cable news programs, Internet websites, self-publishing of blogs, and wikis make an unprecedented amount of information available for us to explore. Yet, today's youth often know less about current events than when magazines were published monthly and news programs were only one hour long. Teachers can easily bring this information to the classroom as instructional resources. Whether it is more traditional broadcast news and newspapers, or Internet-based news programs and archived video, these information sources are convenient and low cost. While many of these current events are news items of common knowledge to adults, they are often unexplored content for students. This sets up the possibility for inquiry and exploration of new information. Current events also provide up-to-date, real-world information to which students can apply the math, science, or language arts skills they are learning.

Any subject area and any grade level can be connected to current events. By connecting lessons to current events, teachers raise the level of rigor and relevance and extend student thinking and application in a lesson.

As a teacher, constantly reflect connecting lessons to current events. This will add relevance and answer the proverbial question "When will I ever use what I am learning?" When spending time listening to or reading news sources, keep track of news items that offer a way to raise the level of student work and learning. Challenge students to look for current events items that can be connected to a lesson.

Pedagogy Perspective

Current Events is an ideal strategy for students with the following learning styles and intelligences.

Sensory Mode	Auditory
Thinking Modes	Concrete-Sequential Concrete-Random Abstract-Random
Multiple Intelligences	Verbal/Linguistic Visual/Spatial Naturalist

What Makes It High Rigor/Relevance?

By making comparisons of concepts, skills, and knowledge to current events and creating new information or predictions of future events, students are thinking at the analysis and synthesis level. By making connections with current events, current conditions, and current data, students are working with real-world problems, clearly high relevance. Students see the connection with what they are learning.

How to Use It

One way to make connections with current events is to create ready access to periodicals and news programs. Make sure the sources you use are current and up-to-date examples that are happening all around us at any given time.

Newspapers

For local current events, use your town or city newspaper. These are stories that are close to home; students can really relate, for these are stories happening in their own backyard. In fact, it might be feasible for each student to have a copy to read along with you. Use the Internet to find out if these events are happening only in your community or in other areas, too.

Current Events Magazines

Using subscriptions to magazines is a great idea. There are many different magazines, focusing on different subjects, to choose from. You can find these magazines by typing in "current news magazines for kids" in an Internet search engine. Some good ones include *Time for Kids* online teacher resources and Scholastic Classroom Magazines.

Internet Links

Place some current events links on your class website for easy student access. These could include the education sections of news websites such as CNN, CBS, and NBC.

Where to Use It

Following are some examples of using this D-moment in different subjects and at different grade levels.

All Grades

- **Blogs and letters to the editor.** Have students read letters to the editor or blogs to stimulate thinking of ideas to use for writing assignments.
- **Universal themes in history.** Have students locate and summarize current events articles that depict universal human themes such as justice, poverty, or peace.
- **Environment.** Have students analyze and present science facts, fiction, and opinions related to local environmental issues.
- **Geography.** Use the mention of states, nations, or geographic landmarks in current news items to encourage students to locate those places on a map. Then expand with branching questions such as these:
    - What is the current season/weather in those places?
    - What are the populations?

  - What are common religions?
  - What are neighboring states/nations?
- **Research, predict, and summarize.** Connect to other D-moments, such as using ***Google It*** to research questions that arise from the article around topics that students do not know about. Also have students make predictions as to what they think will happen in the future because of that current event. Extend current events into the ***In Your Own Words*** D-moment strategy by having students summarize current events articles or news reports into their own short newscasts.

Grades Pre-K–5

- **Mathematics of sports.** Have students make calculations based on a seasonal sports team, such as which baseball team or football team traveled the most miles on a given week.
- **Sequence of events.** When teaching the importance of sequence, select a news story that includes a clear sequence of events. Write each of the facts of the story on a separate strip of paper. Invite students to order the sentence strips to tell the story in its correct sequence.
- **Weather/Climate.** When studying weather and climate, have students pick separate cities and chart weather for a two-week period. Students can use the collected information to compare weather (high and low temperatures, total precipitation, sky conditions, etc.) in different places.
- **Race relations.** After reading aloud the book *Chocolate Fever*, by Robert Kimmel Smith, discuss race relations in the book. Tie this conversation, along with discussions of race relations in current periodicals, to Black History Month.
- **Weekend events.** On Monday morning, discuss with students some events that took place over the weekend. Allow students to categorize similar events and group student stories into common events.
- **World conflicts.** After reading the books *Hiroshima,* by Clive Lawton, and *Sadako,* by Eleanor Coerr, make connections between the events in this literature and current uprisings in na-

tions. Provide a graphic organizer for students to take notes of their analysis.

- **Newspapers.** Review the newspaper with students every morning. Students can cut out articles or report on current events to the class. Relate a social studies unit to an event that is happening at the time. Have students make connections with vocabulary and mathematics that are related to current events articles.
- **Personal Experiences.** Have students reflect back to kindergarten, where they were taught to share and get along with one another. Discuss a war or conflict going on in the world today. Have students use previous knowledge and skills to list the causes and effects of the current conflict; have them make connections to their personal experience and getting along with others.
- **Endangered species.** If students are studying habitats of various animals, have them search for current articles that discuss endangered habitats or endangered species. Students could extend their thinking about animals and habitats by connecting the current events.
- **Compare and contrast.** Select two pieces of children's literature on related themes. Have students read both books and compare and contrast these stories using a Venn diagram. Finally, ask students to discuss the issues in the books in relation to current issues in the community.

Grades 6–12

- **Analyze TV news.** Give students practice in looking for key information and summarizing. Assign students to read three news service reports on the same event. Try to use three very different services, such as NBC, Fox News, and the BBC. Have students summarize the stories, include pertinent facts, and determine whether any article left out important facts.
- **Family and consumer science.** Have students explore the costs of home ownership. Search newspaper real estate classifieds to find three home purchase options and three rental options. Then search mortgage rates and calculate monthly payments for rental and mortgage. Don't forget to add in a figure for utilities and taxes.

- **Graphing data.** Pull information from the news that lends itself to graphing (for example, budget expenditures, population, or number of barrels of oil imported). Provide students with the information needed and ask them to create a bar, line, or picture graph to depict that information.
- **Nutrition.** After a study of nutrition, invite students to plan a healthy menu for a day. Using newspapers, magazines, store ads, and the like, have students find and cut out pictures of foods, arrange them into three healthy meals, and share the results.
- **Compare events.** Compare and contrast historical events (such as war or empires) to current events.
- **Mock debates.** Using prior knowledge and activities, have students relate public sentiment toward the Vietnam conflict to the current Middle East conflict. Have students work in groups to discuss the Gulf of Tonkin resolution, increase in troop numbers, and public perception of success or failure. Have groups debate their views and perceptions and decide whether they support or protest the decisions made in the current Middle East conflict.
- **Business.** When studying types of businesses, students sometimes have a hard time distinguishing what constitutes a monopoly. Have students research when Microsoft was accused of creating a monopoly. Have students research information about the laws regarding the charges against Microsoft. Students have to defend their opinions/findings on why Microsoft should or should not be accused and penalized for creating a monopoly.
- **Historical comparison.** In 7th-grade social studies, make connections between the Guantanamo Bay detention camp established in 2002 and WWII Japanese internment camps.
- **Creating new nations.** Have students read a current article on Iraq's struggle to develop a new government. Then have students use their prior knowledge of difficulties during the United States' Constitutional Convention to compare and contrast the two developments.
- **Compare events.** When studying significant or dramatic events such as Pearl Harbor, have students also identify a current event with a similar dramatic impact and collect pictures from that current event. Then have students compare and contrast the events'

impact on society and that time. Have students write captions for the pictures that they have selected.

- **Science research.** It is easy to find current events that are tied to many lessons. For example, when students are working on genetics, have them find and share articles that they have read or they find on the Internet about cloning and stem cell research.
- **Lessons from history.** When studying Julius Caesar and Roman history, ask students to compare that time period to our current government officials today and the level of support for our president. What are the similarities and differences?
- **Religions and history.** When studying religious practices/persecution in Europe prior to and during the American Revolution, have students compare these two conflicts with current issues between Western religions and Muslim culture.
- **Earth science.** Ask students to find a current event relating to some aspect of earth science. Have them write their opinion or feelings on the topic and share with the class. In 7th-grade science, when studying plate tectonics, determine what percentage of the world population lives near fault lines or active volcanoes. Have students write persuasive pieces to try to convince those communities that it would be benefit them to move or relocate.
- **Business/Marketing.** Use stock market futures quotes to track real investments and have students determine which is the best or safest investment. Have students start with a set amount of money and let them trade daily. At the end of the lesson, see which students made the best marketing or investment choices.
- **Ecology.** When teaching ecology in 7th-grade science, pose a solution or action plan to solve or minimize an ecological issue.
- **Religious persecution.** When studying historical events such as the Salem witch trials and the 1950s Red Scare, have students relate these incidents to current profiling around religious differences and illegal immigration.
- **Genocide.** Connect accounts such as *The Diary of Anne Frank* to recent genocides in the world.

Fix It

Overview

You are familiar with the expression "Learn from your mistakes." That is exactly what this D-moment is about. Students often perceive school as a series of questions and attempts to get the right answer. When a student gets a right answer, there is a positive reward and it will help raise grades; when there is a wrong answer, it likely results in a drop in a grade. But, the event quickly passes, and the student goes on to the next attempt at a question, often without taking the time to analyze the reason for the mistake. It is in the reflection of discovering why the student made a mistake that real learning can occur.

When learning in school is reduced to a trivia contest of recalling facts, it gives the impression that learning is all about the right answer. There is little need to figure out why a student got the wrong answer; it was just a fact that the student had failed to memorize.

In subjects like mathematics, where more complex skills build on basic ones, or science, where fundamental concepts are the key to understanding more complex concepts, students will be stunted in their learning if they fail to analyze the source of mistakes in foundational learning and correct them. Also, there are times when a student may guess at an answer or use faulty logic and still arrive at the correct response ("lucky guesses"). A teacher and student may move onto the next topic, assuming that the student has learned, but the student has not really learned the concept. By taking the time to analyze incorrect answers in a class, students (including lucky guessers) are more likely to reinforce their learning.

Use student mistakes as learning opportunities to reteach; to check for understanding; and, more important, to deepen students' thinking and application of learning.

Pedagogy Perspective

Fix It is an ideal strategy for students with the following learning styles and intelligences.

Sensory Mode	Visual
Thinking Modes	Concrete-Sequential Concrete-Random Abstract-Sequential
Multiple Intelligence	Logical/Mathematical

What Makes It High Rigor/Relevance?

When students are asked to examine their work, particularly work that results in a wrong answer, they have to "analyze," which is a more rigorous thinking skill. Analyzing one's own work requires critical reflection, which is a higher-level thinking skill. Questions and student responses are a proxy for student learning. We can never really measure what learning has occurred, so we use questions, answers, and student work as proxies to estimate student learning. When we engage students in analyzing wrong answers, whether their own or others', we are elevating the level of thinking and reinforcing learning. Questions and answers become tools for learning rather than simply proxy measures to estimate the level of learning.

Students are not necessarily learning when they give a correct answer; they are only recalling what they have learned previously. Students also are not learning when they fail even to attempt a problem they think is too difficult. It is when students attempt to figure something out, complete a task with support from others, or correct a mistake that students are actually learning. This is called the zone of proximal development, or ZPD. In the zone of proximal development, the child is ready to grow cognitively. Working to correct mistakes is actually powerful learning.

There is an element of teaching others when students analyze and correct other students' mistakes. This introduces another aspect of relevance into student learning. Students must apply their knowledge of a concept to discover why another student's answer is wrong and how to fix it. In this work, the student is taking on the role of teacher to analyze student thinking and is attempting to reteach to reinforce the desired learning.

How to Use It

There are many ways to incorporate ***Fix It*** into daily instruction. One of the first strategies is to have students show their work in addition to arriving at the answer. This might include having students write on a board or document projector. By observing the steps in a math problem or balancing a chemistry equation, students find it easier to see where a mistake in logic occurred.

When students help correct the work of others, the entire class gets involved. It is important to not just score the correct answers but to identify where students are making mistakes and to correct those mistakes. This might be done by having students work collaboratively to discuss the incorrect answers.

Whenever possible, try to correct mistakes anonymously before the whole class. Note students' mistakes as you monitor; then put them on the board later, giving students themselves the opportunity to correct them in pairs or small groups. Anonymous error correction is a kind way to deal with mistakes. It is not important who made the mistake originally; the point is, can students all correct it? Perhaps revise the mistake so that even the student who created it does not recognize it as his/her own.

Be sure to create a climate in the classroom that encourages students to try. If the only emphasis is on getting the "right" answer, students may not attempt answers at all for fear of making a mistake. Always give encouragement to students who try.

Initial mistakes are good things, and students need to know that. You might encourage students to make lots of mistakes in your lessons, but new mistakes, not the same old ones again. Say, "I like mistakes because we can all learn from them and because if you don't make any, I won't have a job!" If a student is not making any mistakes, that student may belong in a higher-level class because she or he is learning very little.

Begin by acknowledging your own mistakes. Some teachers worry that students will lose respect for them if they admit their mistakes. The opposite is true: When a teacher makes a mistake and then demonstrates how to handle it by reflecting upon it and learning from it, students gain respect for the teacher. They also learn valuable skills for coping with their own mistakes and become bolder about exploring their own talents and creativity.

Where to Use It

Following are some examples of using this D-moment in different subjects and at different grade levels.

All Grades

- **Reviewing quizzes.** After giving an assessment, hand it back to the students and go over the most missed problems or any gaps in learning that the assessments revealed. Rather than explaining those yourself, engage the students. Approach the students who mastered certain topics and ask them to present one of the sessions that day. Place the desks in small groups or pods around topics on the test. Assign students who did well on tests to be presenters. Assign students who did poorly on topics to the session that is their weakness. The teacher is the facilitator to make sure all groups are on task. Students are free to move to another session once they have mastered a topic. Sessions are 15 minutes long, so students must work together quickly. Students will often use methods that differ from those of the teacher to solve the same problems. This can lead to greater student learning, which is the goal.
- **Grammar.** When teaching grammar, give students incorrect sentences to fix and improve rather than have students routinely memorize correct structures. On students' papers, only flag the incorrect areas; have students figure out what is wrong and how

to fix it. Student errors in writing could either result from a lack of knowledge or be careless mistakes. When students go back and correct mistakes, they can realize that it was either a careless error, requiring better proofreading, or a more significant problem, requiring relearning sentence structure or vocabulary.

- **Reviewing test errors.** Establish a routine when students review their corrected tests. Use these four major categories of errors to identify the source of each error:
    - I know the material, but I made a careless error.
    - I didn't understand the question.
    - I understood the question, but I didn't know the answer.
    - I didn't learn the material well enough.

  Require students to look at *each and every error* on their test, find the category of error, and then figure out how to fix the mistake. Why, exactly, did they make that mistake? How can they avoid making it in the future?
- **Tip sheet.** After completing a unit, have students create a "tip sheet" for future students on avoiding the most common errors.

Grades Pre-K–5

- **English language learners.** In language development, the best way to correct mistakes is to have students correct themselves. Ideally, a student will realize a mistake has been made and will fix it automatically, but that is not always the case. If a student answers a question using incorrect grammar or pronunciation, you can gently prompt the student to revisit the answer. One of the ways to do this is to repeat what the student said, placing emphasis on the incorrect portion; for instance, repeat "I have play baseball," saying it in a questioning way. At this point, the student has an opportunity to think about and revise his/her initial response. You may have your own method of prompting students with a facial expression or phrase that they associate with being incorrect, but avoid saying words such as *wrong, incorrect,* or *no* in response to mistakes.
- **Vocabulary.** When learning vocabulary, give examples of what the word means. Often, requiring students to list nonexamples,

as well, is a way to further define a term and specifically reference those incorrect examples. By listing and eliminating incorrect answers, students deepen their knowledge.

Grades 6–12

- **Proofread writing.** In more extended student writing, have students bring what they believe is their final draft to class. Ask students to exchange papers and proofread, marking all grammatical errors, typos, and instances of common errors on the draft. After students get their own paper back, tell them that you will collect both that version of the paper and a corrected, reprinted version of the paper at the next class meeting. Be sure to emphasize the deduction from their grade if they do not turn in a corrected version of the paper.

Future Think

Overview

Future Think is about directing students' thinking to make predictions about the future. This might be analyzing historical events or current events and projecting the impact of those events into a future time. It might be reading a story and asking students to create an alternate ending for the story or to make predictions about the ending. It might be revising a mathematics problem by substituting different variables and explaining how that change in variables would change the answer. It might be a prediction about new scientific discoveries or a technological innovation.

Pedagogy Perspective

Future Think is an ideal strategy for students with the following learning styles and intelligences.

Sensory Mode	Visual
Thinking Modes	Concrete-Random Abstract-Random
Multiple Intelligences	Verbal/Linguistic Interpersonal Existential

What Makes It High Rigor/Relevance?

Future Think is high rigor because it stimulates student thinking and analysis. Students are no longer seeking a correct answer, but analyzing a number of pieces of information and creating their own solution in the form of a prediction. This has all the elements of higher-level thinking skills, or rigor. ***Future Think*** allows students to use their creativity. Because they have the choice to come up with their own answer, it is highly engaging.

Future Think is also relevant because it asks students to analyze several current conditions and make a prediction. The aspect of creating is relevant as students apply their knowledge to new situations and create logical solutions based on analysis of current information.

How to Use It

Before students can make some predictions about the future, they must build background knowledge. In mathematics, this might be as simple as learning particular math operations; in history, it might be reading or viewing information relating to an historical event. A beginning step can be to quiz students about their acquisition of this particular Quadrant A knowledge. Rather than stopping with the recall of knowledge, move students into thinking at higher levels of rigor and relevance by having them make predictions based upon their content knowledge. This will help to deepen their knowledge and extend their thinking to higher levels of rigor by analyzing that content knowledge and coming up with original extensions.

Do not expect students to give immediate responses when making a prediction. When asking students to recall knowledge, expect students to give immediate responses; however, when students are making predictions, they will need time to analyze and reflect. It also might be more effective to have students work in pairs or small groups to brainstorm, discuss, and reflect on potential predictions, and pose answers. Like most high-level thinking, students will need time to create an answer. This does not have to be an extended period of time; for example, you might shift students into small brainstorming groups for 3–4 minutes.

As a teacher, be prepared for unexpected answers. Try never to give feedback that calls a prediction a "wrong" answer. If a student has failed to correctly include or interpret current information or has made too significant a leap to an unrealistic prediction, compliment the student in coming up with a prediction; then ask the student to revise the prediction based on information that might have been missed or misinterpreted. It may take some time for students who have always perceived school to be about "right" and "wrong" answers to become comfortable with posing predictions.

Having students make predictions can be a highly engaging strategy to increase rigor and relevance and to add student motivation about a particular topic. It also gives them a feeling of being involved in the learning rather than being a passive observer of the learning.

Where to Use It

Following are some examples of using this D-moment in different subjects and at different grade levels.

All Grades

- **Natural resources.** After studying recycling/conservation of natural resources, have students brainstorm what your area might be like in 10 years if these efforts stopped. Have students work in groups to write descriptions of urban, suburban, and rural areas, including illustrations. Have students present ways to encourage more recycling/conservation in the future.
- **Class rules.** Have students come up with their own set of classroom rules. Then have students predict what the classroom would be like if everyone followed those rules. After the discussion, create an actual set of classroom rules.
- **New technology.** Ask students to reflect on a popular technology device, such as a smartphone or digital game, and make predictions about what these devices will be like in 20 years.
- **Inventions.** Have students write about what would be different in our world if certain inventions had not been created. What inventions will they predict for the future?

Grades Pre-K–5

- **Science/History.** Make predictions of the future based on scientific or historical knowledge. For example, if there is less fuel, how will using more fuel-efficient vehicles affect the economy and environment?
- **Reading prequel.** After reading the book *Z for Zachariah,* by Robert C. O'Brien, have students create a prologue or prequel to the book. Students must keep the same era, time, and style. They can use the same or a different point of view but must be consistent or justified. All events must lead up to the beginning of the novel. Details should focus on life before the nuclear war.
- **Reading pauses.** Prior to reading a book in class, give students background information on the subject matter or genre. Then read or start reading the story, and at key intervals stop and ask students to brainstorm predictions about what they think will happen. As you read on, determine which of the predictions come true. Doing so gets students thinking about why one prediction came true and why another didn't happen. Talk about their thought process in making predictions.
- **Environmental impact.** Have students make predictions about the environmental impact if various insect species disappeared.
- **Science inquiry.** When you work with a group of young students and introduce insect life cycles, students might observe small caterpillars grow and change into butterflies. During this process, students learn the parts of the insect habitats and about insects' lives. Once the butterflies are fully developed and released into "the wild," have students predict where the butterflies will go, what they will eat, and what their lives will be like.
- **Invent a machine.** In the study of communities, have students design a machine of the future that must benefit the community in some way. Have students write about how their machines work and how the machines will help people with their daily lives.
- **Emotions in writing.** In a writing assignment, have students write about playing in a high school, college, or professional football game. Have half of the students write about the event

by assuming that they won and the other half write by assuming that they lost.

- **Music.** In elementary music, after students conduct a performance, ask them to set some goals as to what they would like to achieve at the next concert or even by the end of the year.

Grades 6–12

- **History.** Have students read and respond in a critical fashion to Dr. Martin Luther King, Jr.'s "I Have a Dream" speech. Ask, "How would his speech sound today? What would his concerns be today?"
- **Science fiction literature.** After discussing science fiction as a genre of literature, have students describe items we have today that would have seemed to be science fiction 100 years ago. Then have students describe items 100 years from now that would seem like science fiction to us today.
- **Earth science.** When discussing plate tectonics and how the continents are drifting at a rate of 2 cm per year, ask the question "What will the continents look like in another 200 million years?" Form students into groups and have them sketch diagrams of what they think the continents will look like in the future. Ask each group to have students play different roles as recorder, artist, and statistician to make the calculations.
- **Economics/Politics.** Ask students to take one side of a particular current economic or political problem that is facing the state or nation. Have students make a prediction about how this decision ultimately will be made and make further predictions about the impact of that particular change.
- **Career/Technical education.** When teaching a career/technical education course, such as Family and Consumer Science, have students initially create a timeline of important events in that industry. Then have students make a future timeline of the next two decades and predict what they think will be future changes to that field.
- **Scaling up.** In middle-level mathematics, give students a copy of a diagram of the current playground; then have them create

a future diagram based on a problem with this playground. Create problems around ratios by indicating a need to expand the equipment to serve a larger group of students.

- **Experimental data.** In middle-level mathematics, have students perform multiple trials of an experiment and then average their data and make predictions about the outcome of the next trial, using proportions. Have students check their predictions against the actual performed experiment.
- **Health issue.** Talk about the obesity issue. Then have students analyze the current trends in obesity rates and make predictions for the next 20 years.
- **History.** When discussing westward expansion in American history, talk about what the pioneers had to take with them and what they had to leave behind. Ask students to think about being pioneers to the moon and to make a list of which possessions they would take and which they would leave behind. Then compare items from their moon list with the supplies that pioneers took West, noting similarities and differences.

Google It

Overview

The Internet has changed the way we locate information. Google has become one of the most successful companies created in the Internet era because of the ease of use of its search engine. Whenever we need to recall a piece of information, it often is actually faster to search for it on the Internet than to try to recall it from the recesses of one's mind. Google has become so pervasive that the word *Google* has become a verb meaning "to search." The Quadrant D-moment ***Google It*** is about using Internet searches to acquire knowledge. Google is certainly not the only search engine, and other Internet tools could be used to follow these teaching strategies, but all of these D-moment activities involve searching the Internet.

Google is actually a suite of products, many of which help students explore knowledge. For example, Timeline sequences data-related events around the topic being searched. Wonder Wheel creates a hyperlinked visual wheel with spokes of synonyms for the word being searched. Google Books has full copies of hundreds of public domain works of literature. The Voice command functions related to Google make it easy for students with the use of verbal commands. Google also has extensive resources for educators and helpful tips on Internet safety.

Google It is a teaching strategy that extends "teachable moments." The Internet should not be a primary teaching strategy for students but a way to supplement learning when questions arise in student discussion and the answer is not directly available. ***Google It*** engages students to seek answers to their questions using the extensive information on the World Wide Web, making their learning more relevant.

Pedagogy Perspective

Google It is an ideal strategy for students with the following learning styles and intelligences.

Sensory Modes	Visual Tactile
Thinking Modes	Concrete-Sequential Concrete-Random
Multiple Intelligences	Verbal/Linguistic Logical/Mathematical

What Makes It High Rigor/Relevance?

It may seem that using Google as a search tool to locate information is actually about Quadrant A — low-rigor, low-relevance learning, where students are just acquiring information. When completing a short-answer worksheet, students may actually use Google to fill in the blanks; this is low rigor. However, when Internet searches are used to locate information to answer a question that the student poses within a class discussion, it actually has the elements of high rigor. When students are posing questions for additional information, they are actually making the connection between the new information under discussion, their prior knowledge, and questions about what they would like to learn additionally. This has characteristics of high-rigor analysis and synthesis.

This strategy also is relevant because students will routinely use Internet searches to answer questions in the real world. Becoming familiar with the effective use of these tools increases the relevance of their learning. Also, the learning is focused around students' choices, and interest creates a high degree of relevance.

How to Use It

Use Internet searches for the spontaneous questions that arise during class discussions. When students are expected to acquire knowledge routinely, have them do that through specific assigned reading. Use ***Google It*** to extend the learning with related topics and student questions.

Google is much more than a simple search engine. Following are suggestions for making students' searches more powerful.

Use the following features in the search window to create more precise searches.

- Put double quotes (" ") around a set of words to search for the exact words, in that exact order, without any change.
- Search within a specific website by putting the command (site) following the search words, such as searching for Iraq with entries [iraq site:nytimes.com] or [iraq site.gov].
- Use the word OR between search terms and locate sites that have either keyword present. (As a default, Google assumes AND and searches for all of the search words.)
- Use these "More search tools" to display search results in optional ways in Google.
- Dictionary — locates standard definitions for search words.
- Reading level — identifies results as "basic," "intermediate," or "advanced" in level of difficulty.
- Nearby — searches websites physically located in your community.
- Translated foreign pages — provides English translation of websites created in other languages.
- Verbatim — searches for results that contain the exact words you searched for.

Use "Advanced Search" links options under Google results for various purposes.

- Designate reading levels as "basic," "intermediate," or "advanced."
- Designate Usage Rights to find copyright or open source material.
- Activate Safe Search filters to prevent adult content from appearing in search results.

Where to Use It

Following are some examples of using this D-moment in different subjects and at different grade levels.

All Grades

- **Find unfamiliar words.** Have students use Internet search engines to look up unknown vocabulary words or unfamiliar words in reading.
- **Answer questions.** When students ask a question that relates to the discussion topic but is something that they have not previously studied, instead of giving them the answer, show them how to access the Internet and find the answer themselves.
- **Computer adaptations.** Have students with disabilities initiate search functions with Google Voice commands to locate information orally.
- **Use Google Voice.** Help English language learners practice pronunciation while doing searches.
- **Translate.** Use language tools to make it easy to translate text among several languages.

Grades Pre-K–5

- **Discovery research.** After reading aloud the book *Chocolate Fever*, by Robert Kimmel Smith, have a conversation about chocolate and its origins. Have students research chocolate from plants to products and stores.

- **Writing.** Have students read about papermaking or some other process of making common products we use every day. Have the students write a "Did You Know?" on how this product is made.
- **Geography.** Have students explore an African country for a special activity in school. Students learn about the country through songs, customs, and geography. Extend the learning by having students create an African jungle and display some of the mammals, reptiles, and birds native to the particular country.
- **History experts.** Challenge students to become an "expert" on a specific topic. For example, they could be assigned a character in history and be asked to research this particular character and then make a presentation to the class about the person they have researched.
- **Explaining concepts.** When pairs of students are having difficulty explaining a concept to another student, have them enhance their learning by locating a video, WebCam, or animation on the Internet to supplement their explanation.
- **Vocabulary.** When students encounter a word that they think they know and are interested in, such as volcanoes, have them search about types of volcanoes and compare facts with their perceptions of the word.
- **Natural resources.** Have students use Google for Kids to research ways to save water and then use the information to create a pamphlet by adding pictures, bullets, and word art to format the document.
- **Famous people.** Ask students to pick a famous, reputable American to research and to present in a display. Extend the learning by asking students to dress as this famous American and give their "Wax Museum" speech to visitors of their display.
- **Make literature relevant.** When a question arises in a story/reading selection, have students look it up online to find the answer. When reading a literature selection that could be tied to current events, provide an opportunity for students to look up information related to this topic. Discuss the relevance of the information that was retrieved. Allow students to journal about this and to compare and contrast with their own thoughts and what they have read.

- **Student investigators.** Assign two or three students to be "inquiry investigators." When unanswered questions arise during any lesson, refer to the investigators to locate the answer for the class.
- **Answering questions.** Young students typically ask questions. When a student poses a question, instead of answering the question directly, use it as an opportunity to look up an answer. Read the answer to the class and ask students to interpret the answer in their own words.
- **Explain mathematics.** When students in elementary mathematics ask the question "When will we ever use prime numbers?", have students search to find why prime numbers are important and how they are used in the real world. Students then give a scenario of how they or their parents have used prime numbers in the real world, using the information they researched.
- **Geography.** When studying a new country, instead of having students read standard passages, pose questions to students as if you were traveling to that country. Questions could include, "What will I see?", "What types of clothing should I wear?", and "How much will it cost?" Then have students research answers to these questions and report characteristics of the country relative to these questions.

Grades 6–12

- **Mathematical definitions.** When students are learning new mathematical terms or concepts, use Google to reinforce the definitions.
- **Geography.** Present students with the five themes of geography (Location, Place, Human-Environment Interaction, Movement, and Region) and explain the concept of movement. Specifically, concentrate on the movement of ideas and how ideas move faster than ever in the digital age.
- **Cell phone search.** Give students a question and have them use cell phone text messaging to discover the answer. Time them to see how fast they find the answer. Students without cell phones

might function as timekeepers and then discuss whom they would text message to find the answer.

- **Historical literature.** When students read literature with historical references but are unfamiliar with the topics, designate students as researchers to look up information on the Internet.
- **Geography.** When questions arise about geography and locations around the world, use Google Earth to explore more about the location, locate it on a map, and view with satellite imagery.
- **Daily news.** When discussing current events, use Google News to collect daily news articles related to the topic under discussion and to keep up with current events.

How Did That Happen?

Overview

How Did That Happen? is a D-moment strategy that builds on the natural curiosity of students. Curiosity can lead to rigorous and relevant learning when students:

- React with interest to new, strange, or mysterious elements of a problem or issue.
- Show a desire to know more about a topic or a problem.
- Question how a problem is related both to prior knowledge and experiences and to new experiences.
- Persist in researching and exploring in order to know more about a problem or issue.

This type of learning strategy might occur when students ask questions as they observe stories or phenomena that provoke inquiry. It can also be set up when teachers take the time to pose the question in the activities of learning experiences and give time for students to reflect on how something happened. Finally, teachers may also deliberately set up unusual phenomena that trigger student questions, such as the science teacher who demonstrates an unusual and dramatically visible chemical reaction in front of students.

Pedagogy Perspective

How Did That Happen? is an ideal strategy for students with the following learning styles and intelligences.

Sensory Mode	Auditory
Thinking Modes	Concrete-Sequential Abstract-Sequential Abstract-Random
Multiple Intelligences	Logical/Mathematical Visual/Spatial Existential

What Makes It High Rigor/Relevance?

This D-moment is a natural high-rigor/high-relevance strategy. When students pose questions and, more important, research answers to their questions, they are engaging in analytical thinking. This is an ideal high-level thinking strategy.

This D-moment is connected to relevance because students are often making real-world observations that trigger the curious questions. When the student seeks out answers to real questions, he/she is relating that knowledge to the real world, so there is a strong application of learning. In a classroom environment that stimulates asking these types of open-ended questions, students also have choices. This is often an engaging aspect of high-relevance learning: Students are directing their own learning.

How to Use It

The task for teachers is to frequently pose the question "How Did That Happen?" and give students the opportunity to ask that question. Teachers can and should model a curiosity and desire to learn more about topics. There are times in the classroom that a teacher may fake "not knowing" to encourage students to seek out an answer. Most students see through this role-playing; but when teachers encounter something that they truly do not know, they should be honest that they do not know the answer but have a desire to learn more. This models the positive behavior of curiosity.

Moving from posing a question to actually seeking out an answer requires effort. Teachers need to make it easy for students to move from question-poser to researcher. Having Internet resources and other references easily available to students is very important. Look at some of the ideas in another D-moment, ***Google It,*** for ideas on having students research answers using the Internet.

How Did That Happen? is a question. This naturally moves students' thinking to analysis. Not all students are highly curious, and what might stimulate curiosity in some students might result in anxiety in others. With this in mind, the following are six learning strategies that promote curiosity in students.

- **Use Curiosity as a Hook.** Use curiosity as the principal motivator to begin a lesson by beginning with a thought-provoking question or statement. One example might be beginning a lesson on environmental pollution by relating that honeybees are disappearing at an alarming rate and no one knows why.
- **Present Conceptual Conflict.** Students question conceptual conflict when incompatible ideas seem to exist simultaneously in their mind or when information being received does not seem to fit with what they already know. Example: Why does your skin feel cooler when water evaporates off your skin on a hot day?
- **Create an Atmosphere for Questions.** Students need to feel comfortable about raising questions and to have the ability to test their own hypotheses through open discussion and brainstorming sessions. Example: Students question why early Pilgrims journeyed to the Americas.
- **Involve Exploration.** Encourage students to learn through inquiry-based, hands-on, minds-on investigative learning strategies. Example: Create a science investigation about the characteristics of earthworms.

- **Provide Choices.** Provide students with the opportunity to select from several science problems or issues within a specific concept area. Learning strategies that allow selecting a topic are intrinsically motivating and will help sustain curiosity.
- **Integrate Technology.** Provide students with access to the Internet for research and educational technology tools for developing interactive, professional-looking presentations.

Where to Use It

Following are some examples of using this D-moment in different subjects and at different grade levels.

All Grades

- **Problem analysis.** Require students to analyze a problem, connect to real-world situations, and then support their findings.
- **Cause and effect.** Select a high-interest phenomenon, event, or action that is occurring in the world today and that has been highlighted in news programs. Have students use thinking maps to visualize and organize the cause and effect of this event. Use the information from the thinking map to determine why this particular event occurred.
- **Natural disasters.** Have students explain the relationship of cause and effect to describe research related to natural disasters such as tsunamis, earthquakes, tornadoes, and hurricanes.
- **Behavior problems.** Have students reflect on a behavioral problem to analyze how it happened and what the parties involved might have done differently to result in a better solution.

Grades Pre-K–5

- **Cause and effect.** An important concept for elementary students is to understand the relationship of cause and effect. Whenever something happens within the classroom, take the opportunity to have students reflect and analyze to determine ***How Did That Happen?*** It might be a consequence for a student who is not behaving correctly. It might relate to the way an author develops a story. It might involve asking students to reflect on the way they learn basic mathematics skills.

- **Reading.** In kindergarten, use a ***How Did That Happen?*** question to help students summarize and identify the problem that the main character in a book is facing.
- **Science investigation.** When discussing the topic of electricity and magnetism, have students conduct an investigation on "lighting a bulb." Give students a bulb, a battery, and a piece of wire. After the investigation, students use ***How Did That Happen?*** to create/explore a circuit to show the flow of electricity, using their own selection of materials.
- **Geography.** Have students pretend to be a native of any country of your choice. Use digital images to present the culture, population, geography, and economics of the country of your choice.
- **Cause and effect.** Challenge students to analyze cause-and-effect relationships when they observe a phenomenon whose solution is not apparent. For example, "paper bugs" can dance because of static electricity.
- **Science observation.** After students observe a live insect, identify its body parts and tell the function of each part.
- **Persuasive writing.** Use the example of a decision that has a negative impact on students, such as canceling a school trip. Ask students to write about their thoughts and develop a letter to the decision-maker, requesting a reversal of that decision.
- **Cause and effect.** Use a typical event in a classroom, such as a dying plant or condensation on a window, as an opportunity to teach cause and effect. Have students analyze and select reasons for the event's occurring and write answers.
- **Natural events.** Choose a natural event, such as leaves changing color in the fall. Have students raise questions and then research life cycles of living things, weather changes, and patterns.
- **History.** When learning about an event in history, have students discuss and debate what/who caused that event.
- **Analyzing stories.** In pre-K, when reading a story, ask students what made a particular thing in the story happen.

- **Economics.** To teach young students about economics, supply and demand, goods and services, and so on, allow them to "sell" goods or services to other students at the grade level. Questions will arise throughout the sale, such as "What happens to what we have left over?", "If we run out, can we buy anything else? Why or why not?", "Who else sells the same products and services?", and "Why should people buy from us?" These become reflective questions for students to better understand economics.
- **Science.** When introducing science to young students, use natural events that they have experienced to analyze science concepts. For example, have students compare and contrast rain and snow and make thinking maps of the two types of weather.
- **Chemical reactions.** When introducing chemical reactions, have students test, observe, and explain why various chemical agents do or do not clean a dirty penny.
- **Create their own story.** Have students choose a photograph out of a stack of pictures. Have them infer and draw conclusions from the photograph and create their own story. The completed story can be placed on construction paper, on which students will create their own newspaper article.

Grades 6–12

- **Science inquiry.** Give students transparent three-dimensional solids, such as cubes, pyramids, spheres, rectangular prisms, cylinders, and hemispheres. Give students bottles of water to fill the solids. Students pour water into the solids and investigate which solids have the same volume. Find volume of the solids and create formulas for various solids.
- **Current events.** Twitter helped liberate a country in the Middle East, allowing its people to support, plan, strategize, and protest. How is this similar to the American Revolution? Connect the content of current events with past world events, such as the Revolutionary War and Paul Revere's ride to alert the colonists about the British.
- **Helping others.** A lesson about giving to others (the homeless, the less fortunate) can spiral into talking about Haiti and the 2010

earthquake that left many dead, wounded, and/or homeless. Use ***How Did That Happen?*** to continue the discussion around natural disasters and why they happen.

- **Ancient civilizations.** Have students compare and contrast ancient civilizations that they are studying to modern-day civilizations. Students identify the changes and suggest reasons for those changes over a period of time.
- **Civil War.** When studying the history of the Civil War and its impact on the country and families, have students role-play a family member in a specific situation and keep a diary beginning before the war. Have them write about tensions leading up to the war, choose a position, and record their feelings about events leading up to the Civil War.

In Your Own Words

Overview

In Your Own Words is another way to describe the teaching strategy of summarizing. ***In Your Own Words*** is restating the essence of text or an experience in a new, concise form, yet retaining meaning and important information. It requires the ability to synthesize information by putting it into a new format. Students must analyze information, organize it in a way that captures the main ideas and supporting details, and restate it in their own words. ***In Your Own Words*** is similar to ***QuickWrites***, where students write out short summaries. However, with ***In Your Own Words,*** the reporting out is often in oral rather than written form.

Fiction and nonfiction texts, media, conversations, meetings, and events can all be summarized. Students initially want to retell everything they have read, seen, or heard. Summarizing is more than retelling; it involves analyzing information, distinguishing important from unimportant elements, and translating large chunks of information into a few short, cohesive sentences that still convey the original meaning.

Having students reword content allows both students and teachers to monitor comprehension of material. It helps students understand the organizational structure of lessons or texts. It also is a skill at which most adults must be proficient to be successful.

Summarizing integrates and reinforces learning of major points. It not only facilitates recall of the information but also allows the student to see connections and patterns in information that can be useful in other applications.

Students can summarize information in different ways, including deleting information that isn't important to the overall meaning of the text, using synonyms, simplifying, or substituting information with similar meaning. As students practice these strategies, it enhances their ability to understand content.

Pedagogy Perspective

In Your Own Words is an ideal strategy for students with the following learning styles and intelligences.

Sensory Mode	Auditory
Thinking Modes	Concrete-Sequential Abstract-Sequential
Multiple Intelligences	Verbal/Linguistic Interpersonal

What Makes It High Rigor/Relevance

In Your Own Words is high-level, rigorous thinking because of the components of analysis and synthesis. Having students restate things in their own words is higher-level thinking than simple recall of the information. By restating and making the content more their own, students see connections and patterns in information. When students can do this, they are better able to apply knowledge when presented with relevant applications of learning. Research shows that summarization is among the most effective teaching strategies for increasing student achievement (Marzano, R., et al. *Classroom Instruction That Works.* Alexandria, VA: ASCD, 2001). Have students summarize frequently, and they will increase the rigor and relevance of their learning.

How to Use It

Students are so focused on "getting the right answer" that they often want to summarize by feeding back the same text that is in a book. One of the first steps is to make sure students know there is not a single right answer in a summary. Still, a good summary needs to consider the whole passage and restate key points, even if the words are not exactly the same.

A first step for putting information in one's own words is recognizing key words or information. Guide students in locating key words or information and have them practice this step whenever creating a summary.

Remind students about the differences among textbooks, original sources, and nonfiction documents. Most textbooks, particularly science and social studies, are already summaries. Summaries from these types of textbooks are usually just restatements of the summaries in a different form. It is easier to write summaries from original source documents and nonfiction literature, where there is often extra information that can be eliminated to convey the key information. Fiction can be the easiest to summarize because there is often a single theme or purpose buried within much longer text. It may be difficult to find the key information; but once you do, it is easy to discard less important text.

One way to practice writing summaries is to ask students to develop a summary and then give them your own summary. Ask them to describe in writing how and why your summary is different from theirs. Also ask them to describe what they learned from doing this activity. Collect their comparisons and reflections on their learning, not their actual summary.

Occasionally, give students the assignment to summarize for a specific audience. This could be for another student who has not read the material, a younger student, or an adult with a specific interest. Now the student must not only reword the information but also make connections with the needs and interests of the audience. This is a good real-world application of putting content in their own words.

An excellent way to apply this D-moment is as an exit ticket when there are only a few minutes at the end of the class. Generally, students write something brief on a small card or slip of paper and hand it to you or a designated student as an exit ticket when departing the class. You can read these exit tickets quickly to gauge a level of student understanding of the previous discussion. If time allows, students might read exit tickets to the class. The following are examples of exit ticket prompts.

- Name one important thing you have learned today in class.
- Write/Ask one question about today's content that has left you puzzled.
- Read this problem and tell me what you need to do first to solve it.
- Give me one example of how you would apply what you have learned today.

Where to Use It

Following are some examples of using this D-moment in different subjects and at different grade levels (Marzano, R. *et al. Classroom Instruction That Works*. Alexandria, VA: ASCD, 2001).

All Grades

- **Reflection.** Ask students to reflect on their own work and describe one thing they did well and one thing that they could improve on. This type of reflection helps to reinforce the learning and prompts students to think at a higher level.
- **Journaling.** Have students frequently write, in their personal journal, reflections on the daily lessons and reflections on learning.

Grades Pre-K–5

- **Summarizing stories.** Have students summarize a story that they have recently read and compare that story and characters to people in their own lives.
- **Sharing nonfiction.** Group students according to interest (for example, zoo animals, outer space, or pets). Make available nonfiction books on various topics, across reading levels. Have individual students in each group read, take notes, draw pictures, or

make diagrams relating to their topic. Students get together with their group to create summaries.

- **Playing with vocabulary.** Choose vocabulary from the text. Separate your class into two groups. Have one player from each group go to the front of the class and face away from the board. Write the word on the board. The other students have to define the word in their own words without using the word and try to get their player to guess it. The student who shouts the word first gets a point for his/her team.
- **Following directions.** To illustrate the importance of following directions, have each student write out the directions for making a peanut butter and jelly sandwich. Take several of the directions and follow them exactly to construct a sandwich, based upon what the students have written. Have students rewrite their directions when they see that their summary directions left out key information.

Grades 6–12

- **Simulation.** When studying history, particularly the Civil War, have students work through a simulation, with each student role-playing a soldier. As you go through war dispatches about each battle, have students complete the assignment. Ask each student, as a soldier, to write a letter home summarizing what happened, how he/she felt, and how it affected his/her side's effort toward victory.
- **Book review.** When students are reading fiction in English language arts, require them to create a book review and submit these to Amazon.com online reviews.
- **Survival kit.** When studying different climatic regions in world geography, have students create a survival kit for a particular region and justify the reasons for including certain items.

Justify Your Position

Overview

Justify Your Position is a Quadrant D Moment strategy in which students do two things: (1) take a point of view and (2) develop a logical rationale to express that point of view. Students can be asked to justify their position in written form or oral form. When ***Justify Your Position*** is used in a single classroom session, students are often asked to present their point of view in oral form.

This D-moment is similar to ***In Your Own Words*** and ***QuickWrites*** in that students describe personal thoughts and opinions. This D-moment differs from ***In Your Own Words*** in that it must start with students taking a position, making a choice, or having a point of view. If ***Justify Your Position*** is not used orally, then it might be carried out in the form of a QuickWrite.

In order to get students to stretch their thinking and justify a position, you may find it necessary to have them look at a character in a story, current event, or technology from a new or different perspective. In your class, students may have very similar points of view on many topics; however, by creating role-playing situations you can challenge students to look at issues from differing points of view. This encourages them to think more independently rather than repeating a point of view that they may have heard often. It may be easier to engage students in the ***Justify Your Position*** strategy with issues they feel strongly about. As students become more proficient in constructing a logical position for one side of an issue, have them develop support for another side or view of the issue of which they may have been unaware. This type of learning experience will stretch their learning and increase the rigor and relevance.

Pedagogy Perspective

Justify Your Position is an ideal strategy for students with the following learning styles and intelligences.

Sensory Mode	Auditory
Thinking Modes	Concrete-Sequential Abstract-Sequential
Multiple Intelligences	Verbal/Linguistic Interpersonal

What Makes It High Rigor/Relevance?

Justify Your Position is an example of high rigor because students are expected to analyze a situation and develop a logical argument for supporting their position, using available information. There are no correct answers in ***Justify Your Position,*** and it requires original thought to move students from low rigor to high rigor along Bloom's Knowledge Taxonomy.

It is relevant because the use of knowledge in the real world often consists of taking a stand on issues and persuading others to follow your particular choice. Creating scenarios for students to justify their position gives them opportunities to develop their thinking, have more confidence in their opinions, and be able to express themselves in front of others. This is an important, relevant application of education.

How to Use It

In order to put students in a position where they can create a ***Justify Your Position,*** you need to create a scenario in which there can be multiple points of view. Our communities are full of controversy, so you can present students with many civic and social issues that are ideal for taking a position and developing a rational point of view. However, you can also create scenarios, in subjects like science and mathematics, in which students are asked to take a point of view.

Where to Use It

Following are some examples of using this D-moment in different subjects and at different grade levels.

All Grades

- **School issues.** Take a school issue, such as a longer school year, and ask students to take one side of the argument and support their position.
- **World conflict.** Take a current conflict in the world, such as the uprising in the nations of the Middle East. Ask students to take a position in the conflict and justify their point of view.
- **New policy.** After a new policy or event has occurred at school, such as the enforcement of a new dress code or uniform, have students interview the principal for an explanation of that particular policy change. Then have students conduct "on the street" interviews of other students to solicit their reactions.
- **More than one answer.** In several subjects, give students a challenging question in which there are four plausible answers. List the four answers on the board and label each corner of the room with one answer. Ask students to physically move to the corner of the room that corresponds to the answer that they chose. Then ask each group to develop a rational argument that demonstrates why their answer is correct. Have each group report its answer and justification to the entire class.
- **Two sides to the story.** After reading a story about a current events issue, divide the class into two groups and assign each group to one side of the issue. Have students from each group take turns making an argument to support their position.

Grades Pre-K–5

- **Read and choose.** After reading a passage, give students 3″ x 5″ cards. Have students choose what they think is the word, phrase, or sentence that is most important in the passage. On the back of the card, have them write their justification for feeling it is the most important. Go around the room and have each group share important words.
- **Convert fractions.** In mathematics, have students convert improper fractions into mixed numbers and justify their transformation using manipulatives.
- **Select the best government.** When studying different forms of government, have students select the best form of government based upon their preferred criteria and then defend their position.
- **Explain the importance.** In physical education, have students explain the importance of physical activity in their daily lives.
- **Relate cause and effect.** When introducing cause and effect with young students, ask one student to give the first half of a sentence. Then call on another student to give the second half of a sentence. Ask the class to label which part of the sentence is the cause and which is the effect. Have students defend their answers.
- **Take a trip.** Have a class imagine that they are going to take a trip to another country. Divide the class into groups. Have each group select a country, research what it would cost to go to that country, develop a rationale to support taking the trip, and make a presentation to the class as to why group members would like to travel to that country.

Grades 6–12

- **Entrepreneurship.** When teaching entrepreneurship, discuss a current event in which scalpers purchased tickets and sold them at an inflated price. Have students read articles related to ticket scalping and research the various state laws. Then ask students to take a position on the specific issue and conduct a debate.
- **American history.** When studying the Revolutionary War, ask students why they might have been a Loyalist (Tory) or a Patriot.

Students need to consider the perspective of a Loyalist or a Patriot and defend their position or perspective.

- **Current events.** Have students take a position on a real-world issue that impacts people they know. For example, the current economic conditions and resulting unemployment are key issues that affect many. Have students write a letter of support for legislative action on this particular issue.
- **Careers and technology.** In a career and technical education course such as Automotive Technology, an important issue is pollutants and their impact on the environment. Have students take a point of view on a controversial real-world problem related to pollution from a career and technical education perspective and justify their position.
- **English language arts.** In English language arts, after reading a play such as Arthur Miller's *The Crucible,* challenge students to compare extreme religious beliefs today with those in the novel. Ask students to explain what has changed over a period of time.
- **Environmental science.** In environmental science, have students bring in articles about current environmental issues. Randomly assign students to take a point of view; then give them a few minutes to develop a rationale and state a position on this particular issue.
- **Persuasive writing.** In high school English, in persuasive writing, give students a daily writing prompt on a current "hot topic." Students should follow a familiar form to prewrite, plan, and craft a paragraph. Use a prompt that will generate strong opinions, such as "Require high school students to wear school uniforms." Have students share with a partner or small group and discuss their points of view.
- **Constitutional rights.** When studying the Bill of Rights, give students scenarios in which someone's right(s) may have been denied. Ask students to take a point of view concerning whether or not this was a denial of rights and to justify their position.

Learning with Peers

Overview

There is an ancient Chinese proverb that says, "Tell me and I forget; show me and I remember; involve me and I understand." To move students to Quadrant D thinking, you must provide them with opportunities to think in complex ways and apply the knowledge and skills they have acquired. Teaching others allows students to deepen and apply knowledge.

The process of the ***Learning with Peers*** D-moment involves students in learning from and with each other by sharing prior knowledge, ideas, and experiences. ***Learning with Peers*** is a way to move away from teacher-centered instruction to student-centered instruction so that students feel more comfortable with their own learning. This strategy can be used at all grade levels, in all subject areas. ***Learning with Peers*** does not replace individual learning but supplements it and extends learning into higher levels of rigor and relevance while increasing student engagement. ***Learning with Peers*** is a great way to personalize learning in large groups of students.

Pedagogy Perspective

Learning with Peers is an ideal strategy for students with the following learning styles and intelligences.

Sensory Mode	Auditory
Thinking Modes	Abstract-Random Concrete-Sequential
Multiple Intelligences	Intrapersonal Interpersonal

What Makes It High Rigor/Relevance?

Teaching requires thinking, understanding the needs and preferences of the student, reflecting on knowledge, organizing knowledge, presenting information, and checking for understanding. These are all high-rigor tasks. When students are engaged in learning with their peers, they are using many of these higher-level thinking skills. ***Learning with Peers*** is also relevant because it involves the application of what students have learned, engaging them in conversation with peers and drawing upon their acquired knowledge.

How to Use It

During whole-group instruction, the same set of students may consistently be raising their hands to share their answers, ideas, or observations. Other students who are a little slower in processing information before eventually arriving at a place of understanding can feel deflated because their voices are not frequently heard. Rather than a source of frustration, this could be an opportunity to creatively channel the initiative of those who learn quickly into teaching others.

In small-group work in a classroom, at least one student in a small group or pair may become the "tutor" and the other student or students become "learners." In this setting, where they are recognized for their expertise, students often respond well. Some people may argue that quick learners are being held back when they serve as tutors to others. This opinion implies that learning is simply about getting a right answer and moving on. When students tutor others, the tutors are deepening their knowledge and thinking at higher levels. This should be the focus of education. By simply observing different group dynamics, teachers will know when the time is right to employ ***Learning with Peers.***

There are many ways to create peer learning, including using creative games, facilitating peer conversations prior to writing exercises, having joint student presentations, reflecting on learning in pairs, and engaging in tutoring.

Where to Use It

Following are some examples of using this D-moment in different subjects and at different grade levels.

All Grades

- **Writing.** Midway and at the end of a writing unit, have students "teach" their partners the skill they wrote about in their "how to" book. This process not only engages students and teachers but also helps the teacher determine where revisions in students' writing are necessary.
- **Technology.** When students are knowledgeable about a particular software application, ask them to show peers how to use the software.
- **Cross-learning.** Group students in a jigsaw or break apart and teach each other's content from a particular unit.
- **In your own words.** After direct instruction of the new concept, have preassigned pairs of students turn to one another and tell the other student what they have just learned in their own words. Have each student in the pair preassigned, with numbers like *one* and *two* or directions like *North* and *South*, and give specific directions as to which student teaches the other initially.
- **English language learners.** Match native English speakers with English language learners. Using a spiral notebook for recording,

have the pairs of students engage in conversation throughout the year. English learners practice writing skills, and native English speakers offer suggestions about writing, feeling comfortable in the school, and so on. The friendships that are built may continue outside of the learning activity.

Grades Pre-K–5

- **Mathematics.** Have students work in pairs or small groups for reteaching or reinforcing mathematics word problems. Students show one another the steps to solve the problem.
- **Reading.** Have students retell the story of "The Little Red Hen" to peers, using real seeds, flour, and images of the characters shaped from clay.
- **Proofreading/Editing.** Have students work with a partner and share a writing piece with each other. Students exchange and edit their partner's writing piece in terms of punctuation marks, spelling, and capitalization.
- **Student experts.** Label students who grasp a particular concept "experts"; then have them help/teach their peers who may be struggling with the concept.
- **Physical education.** Have students line up in order of their perceived proficiency in a particular skill. Pair proficient students with those that are the weakest. Give the pairs time to practice and teach the technique to one another.
- **Conduct a count.** Give students the task of counting how many boys and girls there are in the class. Select two students, one very able student and another who struggles. Have students decide how they want to conduct the count and then post the results. By working together, students can learn from each other.
- **Manipulatives.** Have students work in pairs, using math manipulatives to explore place value (hundreds, tens, ones). Students take turns showing a specific predetermined number. If help is needed, have partners help each other and check the work.
- **Mathematics.** Have students work in pairs, using manipulatives to "teach" their partner how to sort by a certain attribute. Have students take turns being the "teacher."

- **Riddles.** A student is chosen to be the "teacher." Another student is chosen to be at the whiteboard in the front of the room. The rest of the students have a square dry erase board at their desks. The "teacher" describes a shape in a riddle. (Example: "I have four straight lines. I have four equal sides. I have four corners. What am I?") The student at the front of the class, as well as the rest of the class, draws the answer/shape. The student acting as teacher walks around the room and gives descriptive feedback to peers. When the answer is discovered, select another student as teacher.
- **Number cards.** Have students work with each other to place number cards in correct order. Student pairs name the numbers correctly while pointing to and saying the name. Save time by having sets of cards for each pair of students.
- **Vocabulary.** Assign groups of four students several vocabulary words from the reading and have them look up the meaning of each word. Then pair individual groups to teach one another the new vocabulary words.
- **Checking for understanding.** After teaching a concept in whole-group instruction and before independent practice, have students reteach the concept to a partner. The partner monitors the accuracy of what they are "relearning" and speaks up if a step is missed. The strategy works best in mathematics but can be used in all subjects.
- **Rounding numbers.** Have students work in small groups when practicing rounding of numbers. Give each group a dry erase board with a number line, magnets, and markers. The group comes up with numbers to round and practices the skills of rounding. Students take turns being student and teacher.
- **Performance master.** When teaching a performance task such as playing a musical recorder or demonstrating their facts, create a designation such as a "black belt" in karate for students who have mastered the performance. Have these black-belt students work with others to master the performance. Students take pride not only in their own work but in seeing the students whom they mentor achieve the performance.

- **Reteaching.** In kindergarten, randomly assign a "captain" per table. The captain's responsibility is to explain or reteach his/her interpretation about a particular lesson.
- **Alphabet.** In kindergarten, have students who are learning the alphabet work in pairs to create word books to use for reinforcing alphabet letters and sound recognition. Students may use magazines to find pictures representing a specific letter. Cut out pictures, gluing a book and label. Students can use books for writing sentences and stories. Books should also be in a specific location in the class to be used by everyone.

Grades 6–12

- **Mathematics.** Have students work in pairs after a mathematics assignment to reinforce the lesson. They can check their answers and explain the reasoning behind choices. Another way that students can work in pairs is to peer review written work. They give a compliment, ask questions, and make suggestions for the writer.
- **Physical education.** Have more experienced students teach the beginners what *sets* and *repetitions* mean and which exercises/machines train which muscle groups.
- **Computer lab.** After assigning students in the computer lab to create a word-processed publication, split the class in half. Give students the assignment. Initially work with one half of the class; then shift to the other half. The first half is required to work as a cooperative, as they need assistance, in working on individual steps. They must work within only their half of the class in the cooperative and not call on the teacher.
- **Latin.** A high degree of memorization is necessary for learning Latin. Students use different techniques for this, but ultimately the technique must be applied. Have most able and least able students work with one another as student teachers. This can work both ways, with all students benefiting. More able students become less bored once they have grasped the lesson, and less able students are enabled to catch up.

- **Speech/Presentation.** Have each student choose a topic, give a presentation speech on the topic, and create a document for the audience to take to remember the information. Each student will need to come up with a topic that teaches the class how to do, create, or make something that is interesting and not everyday. Begin by sharing one topic as a model. Be sure to give students a scoring guide to judge the quality of presentations.
- **Mathematics.** Ask, tell, or show students how the concept of mass is used in the real world in various venues. Then have students create a contextual problem applying the math concept. Once students are comfortable with their question, they can share with other students.
- **Preparing lessons.** In place of a lecture, divide students into groups equal to the number of concepts to be covered. Have each group study and then prepare a microlesson about the concept. Use the text as a resource and have each group prepare a formal lesson. One student provides a lecture, one student prepares notes, and one student provides graphs and diagrams.
- **Interpersonal skills.** Have students work in small groups to demonstrate assertive interpersonal skills in given situations. Have the students role-play techniques to be assertive rather than aggressive or passive in challenging interactions with others.
- **Mathematics.** After providing direct instruction in mathematics on a topic such as patterns, break the class into groups of three, where one student is fully confident, another student is partly confident, and a third student is not confident. Have the group develop generic rules for identifying patterns. Make sure that less confident students report from their groups.
- **Warm-up problems.** Teachers frequently use warm-up math problems at the beginning of the class. Select pairs of students randomly to create the next day's warm-up questions for the class.
- **Science.** Have lab partners teach a small group of 9th-grade students the protocol for massing objects on a balance so that they can determine the mass of common objects.
- **Partner research.** Have students research an author of short stories. Have pairs of students collaborate on their findings and then work as a team to create a lesson to present the author's bi-

ography and teach one of the author's short stories to the class. In this learning activity, students should include highlights of the author's craft and style.

- **Health.** When looking at the issue of tobacco versus smokeless tobacco, ask student groups to compare the dangers of tobacco and smokeless tobacco and to present the results to the entire class.
- **JROTC.** Have upper-class students develop and teach a class of first-year cadets a particular procedure such as marching drills, organizational structure, or basic ceremonies.
- **Mathematics.** When teaching something like factoring quadratic equations, where it is important to develop some fluency through repetition of practices, have students work with each other to help reinforce information that they know. Fill in parts of the process of solving problems about which they are unsure.
- **Career/Technical education.** When teaching a career and technical education course such as Family and Consumer Science, have students learn and demonstrate to other students the correct and safe procedures for using tools and equipment.
- **Music.** In marching band, have students take responsibility for leadership in a specific section or group of instruments. Have them practice on specific problems or routines.
- **Technology.** When students are using computer software to complete their work, they may encounter an unfamiliar software application or function. Use other students as tutors to show how to do that particular function.
- **Algebra.** After introducing a particular procedure in algebra, set up six stations around the room. Put students in small groups and have each group create a question to be answered at that station. Students then rotate stations and are asked to answer the questions created by other students.
- **Homework.** Have students write answers to homework problems on individual dry erase boards. Selected students verbalize how they found the answer to their problem. If they have trouble explaining an answer, they could "phone a friend" to arrive at the answer.

- **Mathematics.** Have students go to the board in pairs to solve the same equation (like a race) and explain how they each reached the answer. They can then discuss with the class why their answer is correct.
- **English language arts (7th grade).** To generate interest in reading, have students share descriptions of books they have read. Have them share only the plot, not the ending. This will help to generate student interest in locating and reading the book.
- **Mathematics.** When teaching quadratic equations, form students into small groups of three or four. Give students situations in baseball and roller coaster rides to solve. Have students take turns teaching others in their group how they came up with a solution.

LegoLand

Overview

Legoland is a Quadrant D Moment strategy that involves the use of manipulatives. Legos® are a popular form of building blocks that students can use to make a number of objects. Many teachers are using Legos® construction as more than a diversionary play activity. Legos® can become part of a meaningful thinking activity to engage students in high-quality work.

This D-moment is broader than the use of Legos®; it can be used to describe or incorporate any form of hands-on manipulatives in instruction. Using Legos® or other building blocks and materials extends learning beyond the typical words and language. Using these manipulatives stimulates student creativity and triggers student thinking that involves touch and connection between the fingers and the brain. Often by touching, manipulating, and seeing an object, students find their brains stimulated in different ways, triggering new thoughts and ideas. Manipulatives can be a useful additional strategy for teachers to raise the rigor and relevance in the classroom.

Pedagogy Perspective

LegoLand is an ideal strategy for students with the following learning styles and intelligences.

Sensory Modes	Tactile Kinesthetic
Thinking Modes	Concrete-Random Abstract-Random
Multiple Intelligences	Visual/Spatial Bodily/Kinesthetic

What Makes It High Rigor/Relevance?

Using manipulatives such as Legos® frequently invokes creativity as students "play" with them and experiment with new arrangements. Creativity is a higher-level thinking skill that describes high rigor. With assignments, students are imagining connections between the visual object they construct and the concepts and ideas they are studying. This is an analytic thinking skill that is moving toward high rigor.

Manipulatives also have characteristics of high relevance because students are beginning to apply what they have learned.

How to Use It

Manipulatives are a natural learning tool for writing assignments, providing concrete objects for students to describe. Manipulatives are also excellent for visualizing mathematical operations and concepts. In science, manipulatives make it easy to display or describe objects not visible to the naked eye. Encourage students to use manipulatives in presentations to demonstrate an idea.

Following are some suggestions for using Legos® and other building materials in the classroom.

- Explain to students the connection between using the manipulatives and the concepts you want them to learn. These discussions are essential for first-time users and useful refreshers to refocus all students from time to time. Give students time to explore a manipulative before jumping into an assignment.
- Have set ground rules for using materials. Make it clear that students may be looking for new combinations and creative applications but that there are strict rules for handling and caring for manipulatives. Set up a system for storing materials and familiarize students with it. Use zip-top plastic bags, and portion materials into quantities useful for pairs or groups.
- It is also important for students not to interfere with one another. Step in when a student states that he/she "needs one more yellow tile" and takes it from another group's table.

- Allow time for free exploration. Free exploration time allows students to satisfy their curiosity so they do not become distracted from the assigned tasks. After students have explored a material, ask what they discovered and record their observations on a chart so their classmates can get insights from their ideas.

Let parents get their hands on manipulatives, too. It is important for parents to understand why their children are using materials. Follow up by having students take home materials and activities to do with their families.

Where to Use It

Following are some examples of using this D-moment in different subjects and at different grade levels.

All Grades

- **Scaled replicas.** Students can manipulate scaled paper replicas of the classroom and furniture to organize a suitable arrangement to enhance their work and learning. Provide students with several non-negotiables that must be included. Set aside time for the groups to discuss student and teacher needs prior to grouping students and giving them the manipulatives. Provide a rubric to ensure that students have critical information to evaluate the projects. Take pictures of student presentations and have a vote to select the best one.
- **Special education.** When teaching social skills, ask students to use clay to create an object that represents how they feel when they are very anxious, sad, or frustrated.

Grades Pre-K–5

- **Literacy.** In pre-K, read a story about animals and then have students draw the animal on paper. Then use the Legos® to create an animal. Act out how this animal moves and communicates. What sound does this animal make? What is the first letter of your animal's name? Use sand to make a beginning letter.

- **Models.** In pre-K, during a walk outside, have students observe, record, and take digital photos of buildings in the community. Once the photos are developed, ask each student to create a model of the building that they photographed, using a variety of wood pieces and wood glue. Discuss types of materials that are used to create buildings in their community, such as brick, stone, and wood.
- **Reading.** After reading the story *The Big Orange Splot,* by Daniel Pinkwater, have each student construct a "house" based on his/her own personality. Students then share their houses and explain how the house reflects them. Students compare their houses to others and look for commonalities. Ask students whom they would get along best with and why, based upon their house design.
- **Social studies.** When studying American symbols in 2nd grade, point out that many of the monuments and buildings are in Washington, D.C. After reading stories and researching, have the students build a model of Washington, D.C. and explain what they remember about each of those places. Students can work in pairs to build their model and present to the class what they learned about those places.
- **Legos® map.** Young students can construct a replica of their neighborhood, using Legos®. Students should include houses, stores, schools, and other structures from their neighborhood. Ask student to place the structures on a street map that they create and then to discuss elements of their neighborhood.
- **Social studies.** When reading about the westward movement in 5th grade, have students construct a scene depicted in the story. Have them then explain the scene in writing and present it to the class or a small group.
- **Historical event.** First, tell a story that relates to a historical event such as the Civil War. The story should be very engaging for students. Then ask students to brainstorm everything they know about that historical event. Have students use Legos® to construct an object that relates to the historical event and share a story about the object they created.

- **Create a creature.** Have students build a Legos® creature. Ask them to name the creature, using inventive vocabulary, and explain the name to the class. Have the students tell a story to indicate where the creature lives, what it eats, what it does, how it communicates, how it moves, and what it looks like.
- **Self-portrait.** Prior to having students write about themselves, have them create a visual using a variety of art materials (crayons, pens, glue, scissors, stickers, pipe cleaners, stamps, felt, string, buttons, and so on). Students have to incorporate all important facial features and use their "personality" to create this portrait. Make sure that students use a variety of colors, shapes, and textures. Following the creation of their portrait, they can then engage in writing about themselves.
- **Science.** Have students use building manipulatives to create a habitat that demonstrates how plants and animals are able to survive in the selected habitat.
- **Simple sight words.** Have groups of students use clay to construct simple, familiar sight words as three-dimensional objects to reinforce remembering of these words. Give each group a number of words to remember. For each sight word, have a representative of the group construct the object; then have other groups guess what the object represents.
- **Story characters.** Have students use Legos® or other building media to construct the characters from the story they read. Have them think about how characters have changed. Use the idea of toy "transformers" to illustrate character changes.
- **Vocabulary.** When students are reading and encounter an unknown vocabulary word, avoid giving the answer immediately; instead, encourage students to figure out the word. Have students construct an object from clay to indicate their opinion of the meaning. In addition, have students select specific colors for the parts of speech (green for noun, yellow for adjective, orange for verb, blue for adverb). Then have students check the dictionary for the exact meaning.
- **Principles of design.** When introducing students to the principles of design, give each student a supply of black and white Legos®. Have students work as partners and create four differ-

ent designs for four of the eight principles of design. After each design is made, students make a two-dimensional sketch of the design and fill in the designs with black ink to match the Legos® design.

- **Construct a model.** Have students work in pairs, with one student as the designer and one as the constructor. Set up a partition so that students cannot see one another. Give the constructor a 20-pattern box. The designer creates a design, writes out instructions, and then reads instructions orally to construct a model that is symmetrical. Students then review the instructions and the finished product to see if they achieved symmetry.
- **Area and perimeter.** Have students write building specifications that require a certain area and perimeter. Challenge other students to construct these Legos® houses to those specifications.
- **History.** After studying the voyages of the *Santa Maria* and the *Mayflower,* have students build models of those ships with Legos®.
- **Art.** Have students work in groups to create their own Legos® pictures to represent a famous painter's artwork.
- **Volume.** As students are learning volume, use layers, rows, and columns to show the formula for finding volume.
- **Geography.** When studying a continent, have students construct models to represent the different climate regions.
- **Compare and contrast.** With pre-K students, give each student the same amount of Legos®, including the same shapes and colors. Ask students to make something; then compare and contrast each student's construction.
- **Diorama.** After reading a selection, have students make a diorama to show the characters, setting, and main event of the reading.

Grades 6–12

- **Science.** Have high school students construct a shape or object from Legos® pieces and then create a step-by-step procedure to explain how to build the structure they created. Once the object is completed, ask students to exchange with another lab group to see if they can follow the written instructions correctly and build the other group's Legos® structure. Have students take pictures of the original model and then the constructions made using the directions.

- **History.** After reviewing explorers and their adventures, discuss their ships and the supplies they brought along. As part of this unit, have students brainstorm ideas for their own ship and then build models from wood craft sticks. Once the ships are constructed, test them to see if they will float in water.
- **Family and consumer science.** When studying the topic of food preparation, brainstorm with students the names of kitchen tools that perform various tasks (for example, measuring, cutting, mixing, baking). Give each student some clay; then have students construct visual representations of tools in each category.
- **Chemistry.** Give high school students a set of Legos® that represent the elements of carbon, nitrogen, oxygen, and hydrogen. Ask students to use the Legos® to build models of different compounds.
- **English.** Have students create recycled robots to stimulate thinking and writing. Using recycled materials gathered over several weeks, students make a robot and write about the pieces they used and the purpose for each part. (For example, the water-bottle arms can hold liquids for nutrition.) Have students present their robots in a science-fair format.
- **History.** When studying ancient Greece, have students use the textbook and a set of Legos® to create a map of the Greek islands and show where the important ancient Greek cities are located. Groups share their maps and explain the key that they used. This activity can also be done with clay.
- **Physical education.** Organize students into teams. Give them a few manipulative materials and have each team construct stepping-stones to help their team all cross an imaginary small stream. Each team must get all of its members across a stream without getting wet.

Media Circus

Overview

The *Media Circus* D-moment is about adding relevance to instruction by asking students to make connections between the knowledge and skills being learned in the classroom and the information available in various forms of media. These connections could be to music, television, or movies. Students live in a media-rich world, devoting considerable time to listening to music and watching television and movies. The Internet has not only made access to these forms of media easier; it has also made it easier to share amateur productions of music and video. In this D-moment, students might analyze similarities and differences in the content being studied through the review and selection of various media presentations on the subject.

A second way that ***Media Circus*** adds relevancy to classroom instruction is to ask students to explain what is being studied by developing media forms of audio and/or video as student work. This can foster student interest and add real-world relevance. With modern technology, it is easy for students to produce and share video or audio, often created and edited in a few minutes. For example, students in the classroom can shoot video using a phone or low-cost camera, edit this video to include animation or voice-overs, and complete the assignment in a media format almost as quickly as they might write a paragraph. Just as ***QuickWrites*** (page 123) is a D-moment wherein students have to think analytically, organize information, and write thoughtful answers, with ***Media Circus*** students must analyze information and create thoughtfully crafted answers, but in visual and audio formats.

Pedagogy Perspective

Media Circus is an ideal strategy for students with the following learning styles and intelligences.

Sensory Modes	Visual Auditory
Thinking Modes	Concrete-Random Abstract-Random
Multiple Intelligences	Visual/Spatial Musical Interpersonal

What Makes It High Rigor/Relevance?

Media Circus requires analysis and often creativity, so it has the elements of high rigor in the thought processes involved. Students are not seeking a right answer; they are often seeking to create a logical and appropriate answer in a situation. This D-moment has many aspects of relevance geared to increase student engagement. When connecting learning content to current music, television, or movies that they watch or listen to, students see application to their world. Communicating in video forms is an increasingly popular form of communication. By using this D-moment, students are developing skills with a tool they already see as highly relevant.

How to Use It

To incorporate movies, television, or some other form of video, first select a video that supports the theme students are studying. Start by showing a sort clip. (There are rich video sites on the Internet.) Have students discuss, in small groups, the connection they see between the video and the content under discussion.

Using Video in the Classroom

Video should not be considered a substitute for good instruction any more than watching television in the home is a substitute for parents' supervision of their children. Video can be very engaging, but it also needs to be educational. Teachers can achieve both engagement value and education value by carefully planning the use of video in the classroom.

Planning Before Showing Video

- Preview the video to make sure it is appropriate and useful, and assess the value of the program's support materials.
- Select segments that are most relevant to the curricular focus of the day. A brief video clip can spark student interest or demonstrate a concept, often more effectively than showing a full-length movie. Showing a particular segment conserves valuable classroom time and can focus the lesson for students.
- Prepare the classroom for viewing by checking equipment (monitor, video player, Internet, audio, remote control) and arranging seating and lighting. Lights should be left on as much as possible to reinforce the fact that the video is not passive entertainment.

Part of the problem that teachers have with digital media is fear that students will lose the ability to express themselves in traditional formats, such as the written word. This does not have to be the case if teachers use resources and tools wisely. Teaching students to work with digital media while using traditional skills (grammar, essay format, math skills, and the like) is crucial in creating products that fully express what students have learned. Students are taking the skills they have learned, integrating the new knowledge, and translating it into 21st-century thinking, design, and application. Instead of writing in their journal, students post to a blog. Instead of writing a 10-page paper, a student makes a 5-minute video podcast that posts to a classroom website.

Classroom Applications of Digital Video

- **Assessment of Learning.** Digital video can provide a great way to assess student learning. Remember, the quality of the video may not reflect their actual knowledge. Try to look past the shaky camera work and see the content behind it.
- **Organization of Concepts.** Students have to work with the content and organize it in a way that will make sense to others. This process will help them deepen understanding of the topic and be able to teach it to others through their video.
- **Collaboration.** Video projects are usually created by a small group of students. This type of project is a mass collaboration, showcasing the ideas and talents of all. Students can choose a production position and offer insight from that perspective.
- **Writing Skills.** Most video projects require a treatment (written proposal) and storyboard (descriptions with drawings). This is a great way to reinforce communication skills through effective writing and pictures, and it helps students communicate their video ideas prior to production.

Where to Use It

Following are some examples of using this D-moment in different subjects and at different grade levels.

All Grades

- **English language learners.** Television shows can be useful for teaching English language learners. Show dialogue from popular television shows and then have students role-play the scenes that they have viewed, using the same dialogue.
- **Relate reading to other media.** Relate and explain a TV show, movie, music, or other media related to what students are reading.

Grades Pre-K–5

- **Apply story elements.** When teaching story elements (such as characters, setting, problem, or protagonist), show students a fairy tale and have them identify the various story elements in the video. Students can then apply these vocabulary words to their own writing.

- **Evaluate media content.** Use Meghan McCarthy's picture book *Aliens Are Coming* and a recording of the 1938 radio adaptation of H.G. Wells's *War of the Worlds* to illustrate hoaxes. Lead students to discuss and recognize connections to modern hoaxes on the Internet and elsewhere, which underscores the need to constantly evaluate and verify media content.
- **Examine character traits.** When examining character traits, have students convert the character traits into pictures to represent the trait.
- **Understand sequence.** In reading and writing, when introducing the important concept of sequence, have students analyze recent movies or television shows for the sequence of events.
- **Relate to a problem.** In writing, have students relate a problem from a television show to something that has happened to them. Ask how they handled it or what they would do differently in their writing reflection.
- **Compose with rhymes.** When introducing rhyming to kindergarten students, have them analyze the lyrics in a popular song and identify rhymes. After hearing the rhymes in the popular song, the class can discuss and compose their own song using rhyming words.
- **Analyze conflict and resolution.** After introducing the elements of fiction (plot, characters, setting), ask students to think about popular television shows in which someone gets into trouble. The trouble is called *conflict*. How it is solved is called *resolution*. Have students reflect upon these elements in other TV shows.
- **Solve with manipulatives.** Have students use a video camera to record how they used manipulatives to solve a mathematics problem.
- **Identify story elements.** Have young students reflect on a show that they have watched; identify characters, setting, problem, and solution from the show; and relate these characteristics to a book that they are reading.

Grades 6–12

- **Consumer education.** Have students brainstorm strategies used on television that persuade viewers to buy items. Have students create their own advertisement for consumers.
- **History and culture.** Have students go back in history to life in a particular decade. Have them research television shows from that era. Use this information on television shows to discuss the unique characteristics of that culture, contrasting them with today's culture.
- **Fitness and training.** After teaching students various fitness components, terminology, and training techniques, ask students to watch a sporting event of their choice. Have students describe the various fitness components in training techniques that they witnessed in the sporting event. Then have students work in teams that selected similar sports and come to an agreement on the appropriate related fitness techniques.
- **Safety procedures/technical skills.** In a career and technical education class, have students create a video to describe a safety procedure or to demonstrate proper technique in a technical skill.
- **Economic and social issues.** When studying U.S. history or civics, have students select and watch a television program that provides commentary on current economic, social, or political issues. Have students then summarize what the show was about and suggest a new television show to take an opposing point of view.
- **Elements of art.** Show art students the video starring Andy Warhol, in which he eats a hamburger silently. Have students discuss the video and their reactions and feelings. Ask students whether or not this is "art." After the discussion, have students form groups and create a plan for their own artistic video.
- **Topics in geography and science.** Give students individual research topics related to geography or science. Have them search for video clips from one of several video services and present the video clip to describe and share knowledge about their area of research.

- **Foreign language narration.** In world languages, have students create a video public service announcement on a topic of their choice, with narration in the language they are studying.
- **Rap and verbs.** In world languages, have students create a rap song to remember verb conjugation.
- **Spanish soap operas.** In teaching Spanish, show clips of Spanish soap opera shows and have students role-play the dialogue after watching the clips.
- **Counterculture song.** While learning about Vietnam and the counterculture, have students find a song from the 1960s or 1970s that talks about the counterculture or Vietnam Era. Have students print out the lyrics of the song and explain how the song connects to and describes the point of view of the songwriter.
- **Explore a theme.** When reading stories that have a particular theme (such as bravery), challenge students to bring in videos from home that have a similar theme. Share and discuss these videos and have students vote on the best depiction of the theme. Students can compare books versus media in presenting themes.
- **Correct sports technique.** In physical education, have students tape a video performance of a sports-related task and evaluate and reflect on the correct techniques.
- **Word awareness.** Have students be on the lookout to locate and record assigned vocabulary words. On index cards, students will record when, where, and how the word was used. Students will also demonstrate their understanding of the word by using it in a new sentence. Some sources can be TV, radio, classroom library books, other people, newspapers, and magazines. During the first five minutes of class, ask students to share with classmates the words and information they have located.
- **Video summary.** In science, rather than writing a summary of a laboratory experiment, have students record the experiment on video and narrate a summary.

Original Answers

Overview

One of the traditional assumptions in teaching and learning is that the teacher's role is to guide students to figuring out the single right answer. Teachers give an entire class a word problem in mathematics and then expect each student to work independently and come up with the right answer, by either filling in a worksheet or responding orally. In reading comprehension, students read a paragraph and answer standard questions (for example, identifying character, plot, and purpose). These are typical teaching strategies, seeking a right answer. However, learning at high levels of rigor and relevance is often not about finding a standard answer. Teachers can create higher levels of rigor and relevance by modifying students' questions so they can come up with an original answer rather than a common answer.

By having students seek an original answer, you are challenging them to engage in higher-level thinking, thus creating more rigor. The real world has very few single right answers, so providing students more open-ended questions increases the relevance, more like the way that problems are solved in the real world. In addition, having more open-ended questions allows students choice in what they do and is likely to increase their level of engagement. Students are more likely to work on a problem in which they need to figure something out rather than simply recall an answer for a teacher.

Pedagogy Perspective

Original Answers is an ideal strategy for students with the following learning styles and intelligences.

Sensory Modes	Visual Auditory
Thinking Modes	Concrete-Sequential Concrete-Random
Multiple Intelligences	Verbal/Linguistic Interpersonal

What Makes It High Rigor/Relevance?

Students have to think creatively to arrive at an original answer. Students are logically piecing together the information they already know to try and arrive at an original answer. This takes analytic and critical thinking, solid characteristics of high rigor. With this D-moment strategy, students are creating new and novel information using open-ended questions. These have relevance because problems in the real world are more open-ended. The real world is often not about finding an established "right" answer but about finding the best appropriate answer for a unique situation. Asking students to create original answers replicates more of the real world.

How to Use It

One of the first approaches for teachers to use this Quadrant D-moment effectively is to make sure that the focus is more on the students' development of learning rather than on the students' acquisition of knowledge. Development of learning and acquisition of knowledge are perceived by many to mean the same thing. However, the former is about "learning how to learn" while the latter is about accumulating knowledge in the form of discrete facts. The real world requires students to be continual learners.

Teachers take great pride in their depth of knowledge and want to impart that knowledge to students. Under the pressure of very limited time, teachers try to get students to acquire the knowledge and move on. But learning is more than acquiring knowledge; it is developing the skills to be a continual learner. First and foremost, the teacher's responsibility is to develop learning. When teachers create problems that lead to original answers, students are more likely to enhance their ability to continue to learn.

Students are conditioned to believe that joy comes from getting the "right answer." They receive good grades, prizes, and compliments for a correct answer. These extrinsic motivators influence learning to a degree, but the intrinsic joy that comes from discovering new knowledge is an even more powerful motivator. One of the goals of raising the rigor and relevance of learning is to get students to value the intrinsic joy of learning versus extrinsic rewards. By having more activities in which they discover their own knowledge through original answers, students begin to experience the joy of learning.

As you create questions for students, try to have more open-ended questions rather than closed questions with specific answers. Students will struggle with the vagueness of open-ended questions; however, guidance and encouragement from the teacher will help them engage in these examples of higher-level thinking and learning.

Moving to original answers can also be a gradual transition. You might start with a closed-ended question that has a specific answer. After students have arrived at that correct answer, then pose additional questions that might change one variable or condition. Asking these "What if?" kinds of questions can get students to think more deeply about a problem and to engage in more open-ended problems.

Where to Use It

Following are some examples of using this D-moment in different subjects and at different grade levels.

All Grades

- **Rules.** Have students brainstorm school rules they do not like or that they think need to be fixed. Ask groups of students who want to fix the same rule to create a "better" rule and share it with the class.
- **Mathematics.** When reviewing multiple mathematics concepts, instead of asking a question, give students an answer and ask them to create different questions that yield the same answer. As students generate multiple questions, place these on the board and challenge students to come up with even more questions that yield the same answer.

Grades Pre-K–5

- **Reading.** Read a story together and stop before the ending. Ask students how they would end the story before finishing the story yourself. Alternatively, after ending the story, have students create a "surprise ending."
- **Analyze behavior.** Using the story "Goldilocks and the Three Bears," have students describe the bad behavior of Goldilocks using terms such as *intruder, uninvited,* and *illegal breaking and entering without permission.* Have students then perform a play, "The Nerve of Goldilocks." Analyze Goldilock's behavior from the beginning to the end of the story. Did it change? What did students consider to be appropriate penalties for Goldilocks?
- **Multiplication.** As students begin to develop basic multiplication skills, instead of providing standard numbers to multiply, give the open-ended question of identifying two numbers that are easy to multiply and then telling why these are easy to remember. Having students share these examples will generate several useful rules for multiplying numbers.
- **Machines.** Have students use common materials to create a simple machine that could be used to perform a task in the real world. Students then write an accompanying description of the machine's use.
- **Write an essay.** Have students choose an aspect of a fiction book to analyze, resulting in an essay. Possible topics include the rela-

tionships of the main characters, the importance of setting and how that changes through the book, and changes to the main character and secondary characters. Emphasize "how" and "why" rather than "what."

- **Grammar.** After students have learned and applied an understanding of verbs in writing, have them list their last 10 text messages, bring a copy of a recent e-mail or their Facebook page, or find an interesting newspaper article. They could also pick a page from their favorite book. Have students highlight or list all the verbs used in the document. Then have students work together in pairs to analyze the impact of the kinds of verbs used in each document and to create a classification system of verbs and their use in different kinds of writing.
- **Historical cultures.** As students are studying a particular culture, have them create a game, using recycled materials, that reflects the particular period of time and then share the game with others.
- **Measurement.** Have young students share examples of trips they have taken with their family and estimate how long each trip took. Help them figure out how to measure distances between cities they have visited.
- **Measurement.** When working with measurement, have students measure the area and perimeter of a spider web. Create a spider web out of yarn and oher materials. Have students predict and measure the length of the spider strands.
- **Predictions.** Have students predict how many steps it takes to get from one store to the next. Have groups of students write down their calculations and then actually measure how many steps are required.
- **Physical education.** Have students predict and then actually measure how far they run in a week or month.
- **Rewrite a story.** Ask students to rewrite a story with themselves as the main character and change how the problem in the story would be solved from their perspective.
- **Music.** Have students use a fairy tale such as "The Three Little Pigs" or "Goldilocks and the Three Bears" and write a "sound story" using a percussion instrument.

- **Counting strategies.** When beginning to do calculations with 3rd-graders, have students create routines for counting large numbers. For example, they can count the number of people able to be seated in the cafeteria by counting the tables and multiplying by the seats at each table. Have contests between groups of students to see who can arrive at final numbers the quickest. Then have students share their method for doing calculations.
- **Earth science.** Have students create their own Pangaea puzzle. The Earth's continents once may all have been connected in a "supercontinent" called Pangaea, which was surrounded by an enormous ocean. Using local communities, students create and label their map with fossil clues and cut out tectonic plates. After the puzzles are created, have students exchange and put together the puzzles and give them original names.
- **Learning language.** Give students half of a phrase and have them create a question ending. Then, from the same half-phrase, have them create a new statement that has an answer statement ending. Have them repeat these phrases and use proper dialogue inflection.
- **Combining shapes.** Have kindergarten students take simple common shapes and combine the shapes to create something new.
- **Mathematics and life.** In kindergarten, when introducing the concept of patterns in mathematics, have students describe a life pattern (something that they do every day in a routine). Students can share their routines and listen for the patterns. Then students work with manipulatives to create patterns and compare and contrast patterns with other students.

Grades 6–12

- **Geometry.** Instead of asking students to identify the third angle size in a triangle with one angle of 30° and another angle of 50°, ask students for three possible angle sizes in a triangle that has at least one narrow angle. For another example, instead of asking the total of 35 plus 17, say, "I am thinking of two numbers with a total of 51." Doing so helps students recognize that sometimes there are multiple right answers.

- **Predictions.** Have students calculate and convert the batting average for a professional baseball player as percentages and fractions. Based on this information, have students predict how many hits the player will accumulate in the next five games. Have students monitor progress, look up statistics, and compare actual performance to their predictions.
- **Equations.** When introducing basic equations in 8th grade, have students identify an activity or decision that they make that can be converted into a two-step equation, such as determining how much time to devote to practice of a sport or counting calories in their diet. Students will explain the problem to the class; then the class will help create and solve the equation.
- **Solar System.** After studying the solar system, have students create their own planet. Their planet can be any shape other than a sphere. They then write about their planet, including surface area, climate, life, place in the solar system, and number of moons.
- **Interdisciplinary.** Start with a large-volume food item such as a 3-lb. jar of peanut butter-filled pretzels. Create a series of interdisciplinary questions involving English, math, science, and social studies.
    - In English, students write an essay on ways to determine how many pretzels there are in this unopened jar (by mass, area, and so on).
    - In algebra and geometry, students implement the process as best they can and determine the number of pretzels in the jar.
    - In science class, students determine the number of pretzels in the jar, using mass and scales to calculate how many pretzels are in the jar.
    - In social studies, students research the history of the pretzel and the peanut and peanut butter around the world.
    - The winning team gets the jar of pretzels, to do with whatever they wish (probably eat them all), and a certificate of accomplishment.

Overview

QuickWrites are short writing exercises that ask students to think through the concepts on which they are working. It is a way to provide order to their thoughts, or to shape a meaning out of a jumble of new ideas and notions. Students are asked to think logically and are encouraged to personalize their learning at that moment.

QuickWrites is, first and foremost, a thinking and learning technique that also develops and improves the quality of student writing. Usually, these writing tasks are short and appealing. They energize students and encourage new thinking.

Prompted *QuickWrites* promote daily rigorous thinking. If carefully designed, they provide opportunities for exploring students' ideas about concepts being studied, clarifying misunderstandings, anchoring learning in long-term memory, and building content-specific vocabulary. Oral sharing of *QuickWrites* offers the opportunity for an exchange of thoughts among the students and direction for future instruction for the teacher.

QuickWrites are not about giving a specific correct answer. They most often ask for personal reflection, but they can also seek an opinion, probe for application, stimulate imagination, or request justification.

Pedagogy Perspective

QuickWrites is an ideal strategy for students with the following learning styles and intelligence.

Sensory Modes	Visual Tactile
Thinking Modes	Concrete-Sequential Abstract-Sequential
Multiple Intelligence	Verbal/Linguistic

What Makes It High Rigor/Relevance?

Writing allows students an opportunity to make critical mental connections between their thought processes and the content to be learned. It forces students to focus their thinking and to carefully analyze material. Writing increases retention of information because it forces the learner to take time to carefully analyze and organize the subject matter.

QuickWrites provide teachers with an effective way to assess the understanding of all learners; they also help students focus on critical thinking and encourage application of learning. ***QuickWrites*** are open-ended tasks with an element of creativity, one of the characteristics of high rigor.

QuickWrites provide students an opportunity to actively engage with course content. Students who write in response to the material they have learned begin to:

- think independently
- develop insight
- explore thoughts and feelings
- develop intellectual courage
- reason logically

- follow the thread of the lesson in their minds
- visualize a concept and then make it more concrete
- apply learning beyond the classroom

How to Use It

QuickWrites can be used before, during, or after instruction. Following are prompts for typical ***QuickWrites*** activities.

To Begin Instruction

- What do you already know about this?
- What questions do you have from your reading?
- Write one key point from yesterday's lesson.
- What is something important for you to know about this topic?

During Instruction

- What do you think about this information?
- How is this like _____ ?
- What is a significant question you would ask? Why?
- What do you think will happen next?
- Identify a potential problem or issue.

After Instruction

- What is something important you learned today?
- What do you think are the two most important points?
- Write three things you would say to explain this to a younger child (or adult).
- What did you do to participate today?
- What would you like to know more about?
- What did you enjoy and/or not enjoy about this discussion?
- What is something you are doing to help yourself learn?

- What is something you have accomplished since we began this topic?
- What do you think about this idea/topic?
- What do you not understand?
- How could you use this to _____ ?

Where to Use It

Following are some examples of using this D-moment in different subjects and at different grade levels.

All Grades

- **Read and reflect.** Have students read content for a certain length of time (5–10 minutes); then have students write for 5 minutes about details from the reading or questions that they have about what they read.
- **Keep a journal.** Give each student a reflection journal. At the end of each day, their ticket out is to write one thing they learned or questions they were left with and how they would find the answers to those questions.
- **Connect the learning.** Develop a routine of writing at the beginning of the class and at the end of the class. These might be called "Write Now" and "Wrap Up." The Write Now is typically used to activate prior knowledge or remind students of the concept covered in an earlier lesson. The Wrap Up, another quick prompt, usually has students reflect on the content they learned in class that day and make connections to other material that they have learned in class.
- **Track your understanding.** Have students become accustomed to "beginning, middle, and end" writing. At the beginning of a lesson, introduce the concept and have students write about what they think it means. After the concept is introduced, have students write about what they have learned so far and ask questions or say what they will still need to understand. At the end, have students write what was interesting about the concept and how they can relate it to their own life.

- **Blog your reactions.** In language arts, after reading a piece of literature, have students blog reflections. Ask students to comment on other students' blogs.
- **Tweet it.** Have students use micro-blogging on Twitter with a maximum of 140 characters.
- **Connect the issues.** There are several family television shows that portray typical student challenges. Show video clips from the shows or ask students to watch shows. Then have them complete quick writing assignments, reflecting on the issue and its connection to themselves or their friends.
- **Debate silently.** Use a silent debate, in which students respond to a two-sided or controversial aspect of the lesson by forming pairs. One member of the pair will support one side of the issue; the other member will support the opposite side. Each member writes one statement to support his or her side on a piece of paper. Then the papers are exchanged, and the individual student responds to the specific argument made by the opposing partner. The papers are silently handed back and forth to each other, with comments added to each other's arguments as they develop.

Grades Pre-K–5

- **Take a sensory field trip.** When studying the senses in elementary school, take students on a quick field trip outside of the school and have them write about what each of their senses experienced on the outside excursion.
- **Reflect on learning.** Have students reflect on the content of their learning at the end of each day and how they might use what they have learned.
- **Play "Beat the Author."** Show students a snippet of writing on the board. Have students work in groups and rewrite and discuss why the piece that they have written is better than the author's.
- **Recall the lesson.** After a math lesson, ask students to write for 1–3 minutes about anything related to the previous math lesson.
- **Track your progress.** Have students write for 5 minutes at the end of math class. Through writing, they can discuss something

new they learned, reveal something still difficult for them to understand, or give an original example with a solution in real-world application. Give them choices as to what to write, sometimes giving specific prompts.

- **Create a historical marker.** In social studies, ask students to create a historical marker to be placed beside a highway, next to a building, and so on, that points out the historical importance of that particular place. By writing historical markers, students learn how to condense information, highlighting just the most significant details, as well as how to summarize, into one concise statement, the lasting impact of an event.

Grades 6–12

- **Recalling and summarizing.** Begin the class with 5 minutes of student writing on yesterday's lecture or readings.
  - To check for learning, stop the lecture for a "quick write" about the meaning of their preceding statement.
  - At the end of a science lab, ask students to give a 5-minute recap on what transpired during the experiment, what worked, and what went wrong.
  - Have math students write a quick process explanation about solving the new equation.
  - Have social studies students write their thoughts and beliefs on the First Amendment while discussing the Bill of Rights.
- **Daily writing prompts.** In 7th-grade language arts, as an effort to keep students constantly writing, use daily writing prompts around fun topics. Topics can range from "It's Popcorn Day. Create a new flavor of popcorn!" to "Paper money was first used in China, about 1,200 years ago. Create your own new paper money!" Have students share their ideas in this stress-free creative writing assignment.
- **Advertising copy.** In social studies, after studying about a particular time period in history, ask students to recreate the life of the common citizen by imagining what types of goods or services might be required at that time in history. Then, have students write an advertisement for publication in a newspaper or flyer.

- **Applying math concepts.** Here are some prompts for application of mathematics that will increase relevance and reflective thinking.
  - What is the easiest way to determine whether the solution to a multiplication problem will be a positive or a negative?
  - Which is easier to use: percentage or ratio? Why?
  - Describe a real-life use for what you have learned over the past two weeks.
  - How would you go about finding the area of a circle?
  - Describe one similarity and one difference between ratio and percentage.
  - Explain how pi (π) is used in geometry and discuss one fact about it.
  - What are the relationships among radius, chord, diameter, and circumference?
  - Which would be better to use in planning the purchasing of food for a restaurant: ratio or percentage?

Quiz Show

Overview

Quiz Show is a Quadrant D moment strategy that guides students in formulating meaningful questions about material they have learned. Just as in some television game shows, "contestants" are asked a series of questions to demonstrate their knowledge. Students are often asked questions in the form of tests or worksheets, or as part of direct instruction. In an effort to raise the level of rigor and relevance, however, *Quiz Show* has students create the questions. Students can imagine that they are the teacher or, more interestingly, the producer of the quiz show. Using the content knowledge they have acquired, students must create appropriate questions.

Pedagogy Perspective

Quiz Show is an ideal strategy for students with the following learning styles and intelligence.

Sensory Modes	Visual Auditory
Thinking Modes	Concrete-Random Abstract-Random
Multiple Intelligence	Logical/Mathematical

What Makes It High Rigor/Relevance?

When students are asked to create the question, rather than simply recall an answer, they must engage in higher-level analytical thinking. Students must craft a clear and precise question that relates to the subject under consideration if they are to elicit a reasonable answer. They also must be creative, sometimes coming up with an original solution in the form of a question. This strategy is rigorous because of the higher-level thinking that students must engage in — higher than that required in simply giving an answer. The students who ask the questions have to be prepared to analyze and evaluate the answers to judge whether they are correct or incorrect.

This strategy is also relevant because teaching others is a real-world task. Students must take into consideration the context in which the question will be answered; they must consider the characteristics of the other students or the situation in order to design appropriate questions. All of these complex elements create a real-world environment that is high in relevance.

How to Use It

In direct instruction, students are typically asked to read material, view a video, or listen to a teacher presentation. Following this direct instruction, students are often asked questions to determine their acquired knowledge. Direct instruction that follows this pattern is often routine and boring; often, only one or two students are called on out of the entire group. Instead of asking students questions, collecting worksheets, or calling on individual students, the teacher can engage all students by challenging them to create their own questions. Give students parameters for these questions, such as the types of questions, the content to be included, and the ways they will be used. Engage the entire class by creating pairs or triads of students who will share their questions. Students can take turns asking each other questions. The value of having a third person in the group is that the third person can act as an arbiter to determine whether a question is fair or an answer reasonable.

This type of learning situation requires students to use their creativity to rise to the challenge of questioning their fellow students. Engaging in ***Quiz Show*** and creating questions help to reinforce students' knowledge and understanding of the content. If they have not acquired the content, they will have great difficulty developing effective questions.

You can create even more engaging and interesting scenarios for students by asking them to role-play a specific ***Quiz Show*** game in which they are the game designers or creators. A variation of ***Quiz Show*** is creating a *Jeopardy!*-type game, in which students create detailed answers and "contestants" respond in the form of questions that demonstrate acquired knowledge. This may become too complex for some students unless they are already familiar with this particular game format. You can create a team quiz bowl competition, using student questions. Students can be very motivated around competitions and challenges, so use this motivational aspect to engage students to think in complex ways about the content you want them to learn.

Where to Use It

Following are some examples of using this D-moment in different subjects and at different grade levels.

All Grades

- **Game show questions.** Have a small group of students create questions for contestants to answer in a game-show style.
- **Content questions.** Have students work in triad groups to ask each other questions on content.
- **Varied difficulty questions.** Have students work in groups to come up with items about broad topics such as state history. There will be items about geography, animals, plants, history, and economy. The activity will be presented in a format similar to *Jeopardy!*, with five progressively more difficult questions per category and answers expressed in question form.

Grades Pre-K–5

- **Partner discussion.** After doing a read-aloud and asking questions related to the text, ask students to sit with their partners and answer questions. Then ask students to repeat the partners' answers and explain why they agree or disagree.
- **Real-life math.** Give students a basic area problem with a diagram. Have students write their original problem from a real-life situation in which measuring this area or perimeter would be important.
- **Data display.** Have students collect data and display it on a bar graph. Then have students create questions based upon their graph, omitting parts of the data.
- **Pizza fractions.** After a unit on fractions, have students create word problems around a visit to a pizza shop. Students describe their pizza order (for example, toppings). Students ask their audience to provide the fractional representation of the pizza, using fractions.
- **Author's purpose.** After identifying the author's purpose for a selected reading, have students begin to generate their own paragraphs and have their partners identify the purpose.
- **Math quiz.** Have students create a quiz show reflecting current mathematics topics, such as fractions.
- **Rags to riches.** Use the structure of the game *Rags to Riches* as an assessment. Have students create a math question with an answer. Then have students form groups of three to discuss, change, or clarify questions. The group picks two of the best questions for you to enter into the game, to be played by students.
- **Softball catch.** At the end of the day, each student takes turns throwing a softball, representing a local sports team. When the student throws the ball to another student, the "pitcher" gets to ask a question of the "catcher." A correct answer earns one point toward a prize.
- **Third grade challenge.** Follow the format of the television game show *Are You Smarter Than a Fifth Grader?* Have students come up with their own questions and invite upper-grade students to

come at a certain time during the day. Have all 3rd-grade students prepare to welcome the older students to class by singing *Are You Smarter Than a Third Grader?* The older students will choose a 3rd-grade student and, in turn, will be asked a question. All 3rd-graders have a whiteboard to respond. If the student answers the question correctly, he/she receives a sticker that says, "I'm smarter than a third grader."

- **Sticky note *20 Questions*.** A variation of *20 Questions* is to have the student write a word or phrase on a sticky note related to the topic being studied. Place the note on another student's back. The student has to guess the word on his or her back by asking others questions that are answered by either *yes* or *no*.
- **Local history and culture.** When studying local history and culture, have the students create a *Jeopardy!*-type quiz show and develop questions at the appropriate level by working in their small groups.
- **Vocabulary act.** When learning vocabulary with kindergarten-age English language learners, have students act out different words while other students guess the word.
- **Grocery ads.** When working in mathematics, give students the grocery section of a newspaper and have them create word problems using information from the newspaper.
- **Cause and effect.** Have students make up their own cause-and-effect activities about a story they are reading, using a chart. Have them explain why it's important to understand cause and effect; relate that to understanding literature.
- **Interview questions.** In music, ask students to think of their favorite musician or band; then have them create 10 questions that an interviewer might ask this musician or the band members. Ask students to use the Internet and other resources to learn the answers to those questions.
- **Puzzler.** Have students create a mystery puzzler. Students use key concepts and phrases connected to vocabulary words to write a puzzler that others have to solve. Example: I'm wanted by all, can be used in any physical state, and have only two elements. Answer: water.

- **Outburst.** Divide the class into 3 or 4 groups. Using the format of the game *Outburst*, have the groups work together to list 10 questions under a given category. Groups then compete against one another to see who can answer the most questions in the other team's category.

Grades 6–12

- **Complex area problem.** Give students a complex area problem in mathematics that includes multiple shapes; then ask them to suggest multiple ways to solve the problem.
- **Square roots and quadratic equations.** When simplifying square roots, put the answer in simple radical form. Ask students to come up with their own challenge, solve it, put the answer on another piece of paper, and challenge their partners to see if they can solve it. Use this in factoring quadratic equations. Challenge students to come up with their own expression, factor it, and see if their partner will be able to do the same. Extend this activity by having students graph the parabola and show the vertex, axis of symmetry, and at least two points that are symmetric over the axis of symmetry.
- **Civil War review.** After a teacher lecture, guided reading activities, worksheets, simulations, and culminating projects, ask students to create questions to be used in a Civil War *Jeopardy!*-type game. This game could be used as a review for the end of the unit test. Students work in small groups in class and write items using their social studies books, worksheets, mind maps, and notes collected throughout the unit.
- **Exponents.** Have algebra students create a game that practices problems involving rules of exponents. They provide the rules, gameboard and game pieces, problems, and solutions. The winner of the game is the one with the most knowledge about exponents.
- **American Revolution.** Have students work in groups to formulate questions about the American Revolution to give to other groups. Students use their notebooks and textbook projects as reference tools to answer questions from other groups.

- **Geometric concepts.** In geometry, have each student create at least three questions involving a geometric word or concept covered in class. They could pose their questions as multiple-choice, fill in the blank, true/false, open-ended, and so on. Students face off in pairs to answer questions. Students may use visuals as part of their questions.
- **Any topic.** Play the game *20 Questions* and have a student competition in which you pick an overall topic or subject. Ask students to select an answer; then have other students ask no more than 20 *yes* or *no* questions to focus in on the answer.
- **Career exploration.** When focusing on career exploration and introducing students to careers and career preparation, have students create a *Jeopardy!*-type game show with questions related to each particular career. Students research a career and create appropriate questions.
- **Language study — verbs.** When studying verb conjugation and different tenses in world languages, group students into teams and create a different ***Quiz Show*** for each verb tense. Have each team run through the ***Quiz Show***; provide prizes for the winning team.
- **Language study — vocabulary.** To reinforce vocabulary in world languages, have students design flash cards, based upon the content of the lesson, to be used for review.
- **Short stories.** After reading a short story in English language arts, give groups of students question stems and have them create two questions and four answer choices per question. When every group has completed the task, rotate the cards with the questions through all groups. Each group answers all the questions and then, as a class, discusses correct answers and justifications.
- **Computer applications.** When students are studying the use of digital slideshows in computer applications, they can create a nonlinear product by creating a branching question-and-answer application. Have students use questions and content from their math, science, social studies, and English classes.
- **Gameboard geometry.** Have students create a gameboard to review concepts in geometry.

Remind Me

Overview

Remind Me is a D-moment strategy that challenges students to develop creative techniques to memorize or quickly recall information. Memorization is a legitimate and important part of a student's education. With the introduction and pervasive use of the Internet, some people advocate that there is little need to memorize, for anyone can quickly look up the answer to any question. The Internet is vast, fast, and easy to use, but there are still situations in which it is better to have the knowledge in your own mind rather than taking time to look things up. When engaged in a persuasive conversation, having data and statistics that you can cite immediately is powerfully influential. When performing routine technical tasks, like troubleshooting an engine or taking a patient's blood pressure, it is far more productive to have the procedures committed to memory than it is to look them up every time.

The traditional route to memorization is through rote repetition until the information is firmly planted in memory. Memorizing through repetition takes a great deal of time and is boring to students. Students become less engaged in learning when using rote memorization. By introducing the D-moment of ***Remind Me,*** you can challenge students to come up with creative ways to recall essential information. They will develop habits of thinking that will enable them to learn and memorize, on their own, whatever they need to know. These habits will translate to skills for lifelong learning.

Pedagogy Perspective

Remind Me is an ideal strategy for students with the following learning styles and intelligences.

Sensory Mode	Visual
Thinking Modes	Abstract-Sequential Abstract-Random
Multiple Intelligences	Verbal/Linguistic Logical/Mathematical

What Makes It High Rigor/Relevance?

While citing statistics and performing routine skills are examples of low rigor, the process of creating techniques to be able to recall this information is actually a high-rigor skill that requires analysis and creativity — certainly highly relevant in any learning situation. The actual knowledge may be low rigor and low relevance, but students need to be fluent in its recall and application. For example, a student performing a musical piece needs to recall notes fluently when reading the music, or a student playing a sport needs to have committed to memory the rules of the game before taking to the field. Techniques for remembering information are highly relevant in every subject area.

Remembering becomes high rigor when students create their own techniques to recall essential information. By forming their own stories, similes, lists, or graphic organizers, students are engaged in high rigor through analysis and creativity.

How to Use It

There are three main components to be considered in memorization:

- Using multiple senses
- Making an association interesting or familiar
- Associating new items with something already known

Multiple-sensory instruction and interesting, relevant instruction will aid in memory. In addition, the use of memorization techniques, or mnemonics, creates associations that will enable students to recall critical and important information.

Memorizing does not mean comprehending. Students might memorize dates for a history class or formulas for a math class, but they also need to understand why a date or a formula is significant to the key ideas of the lesson. Before spending vast amounts of time having students memorize details, ask if it would be better to step back and focus on overall comprehension of the big picture. Why it is important? How does it connect to other knowledge? Just because a student recalls the correct information, it does automatically signal an understanding of that information. It may be necessary to use other strategies to check for understanding when that is the important learning objective.

Here are a few general tips on the use of memory strategies to share with students:

- Creative or silly mnemonics often work best because they are easy to remember. Exaggerate size and choose unlikely functions for the image.
- Create your own mnemonics, based on your own vivid pictures.
- Use positive, pleasant images. The brain often blocks out unpleasant ones.
- Closing your eyes while trying to visualize an image or story will make it more vivid.
- Be humorous! Funny or peculiar things are easier to remember than normal ones.

- Symbols (red traffic lights, pointing fingers) can be used in mnemonics. The age-old technique of tying a string around your finger really does work.
- Vivid, colorful images are easier to remember than drab ones.
- Your mnemonic can contain sounds, smells, tastes, touch, movements, and feelings as well as pictures.
- Bringing three dimensions and movement to an image makes it more vivid. Movement can be used either to maintain the flow of association or to help remember actions.
- Use a unique location for each list to separate similar mnemonics. By setting a mnemonic story in a particular location and clearly using that location as a background, you can separate it from a different mnemonic, set in a different place.
- When learning new vocabulary words, use a mnemonic to remember the terms.

Lists and graphic organizers can be useful aids in recalling complex information. Graphic organizers are particularly useful in this D-moment. They allow students to use their creativity to design a display of essential information in a way that is easy for them to recall.

Where to Use It

Following are some examples of using this D-moment in different subjects and at different grade levels.

All Grades

- **Mnemonics.** Have students create their own mnemonics. Share these in groups and with the whole class. Have students record at least three options for the mnemonics in their notebook.
- **Graphic organizers and concepts.** Have students create graphic organizers to show relationships between important concepts.
- **Graphic organizers and relationships.** Have students create graphic organizers to remember characters in a story and the relationships among characters.

Grades Pre-K–5

- **Math mnemonics.** Have students develop mnemonics for the order of operations in mathematics, such as "Please Excuse My Dear Aunt Sally" (Parentheses - Exponents - Multiplication - Division - Addition - Subtraction).
- **Vocabulary and sign language.** Have young students learn and use sign language when beginning to use vocabulary.
- **Math stories.** Read to students the book *Sir Cumference and the Isle of Immeter*, by Cindy Neuschwander, which teaches students the relationship among radius, diameter, and circumference. Have students create their own stories to remember mathematic concepts.
- **Dramatizations.** When reading stories to young children and helping them to recall characters in the story, have them create and perform dramatizations that will help them remember the names of the characters.
- **Process recall.** When teaching young students personal hygiene and hand-washing, have them work in pairs to teach one another. Review each of the steps to make sure that partner students complete all the steps in hand-washing. Have each pair of students come up with a way to remember all of the steps in effective hand-washing.
- **Hand gestures.** In science, have students create hand gestures or motions to explain or remember difficult science concepts (for example, speed equals distance divided by time).
- **Metaphors.** In physical education, have students come up with a metaphor to remember the rules in a sport, such as kickball.
- **Decimal dance.** When teaching students to multiply decimals, help them remember to mark the decimal point by using the decimal dance. At the board, work out the product of the numbers and exaggerate the motion of counting decimal places until all places are accounted for. By calling this *The Decimal Dance,* students remember to account for decimal place value after multiplying decimals.

Grades 6–12

- **Geometry jigsaw.** Have students create a jigsaw activity for a 10th-grade geometry lesson on a topic such as special segments of triangles.
- **Conjunction mnemonic.** In English, have students learn the mnemonic for the seven coordinating conjunctions (**F**or, **A**nd, **N**or, **B**ut, **O**r, **Y**et, **S**o = **FANBOYS**).
- **Best strategies.** Have students think metacognitively about what they do as they are reading, to help them understand their reading processes and the strategies that work best for them. Have students share with the class and make a list of the reading strategies they used, noting the differences among them.
- **Personal pledge.** To reinforce the meaning and historical significance of things like the Pledge of Allegiance, have students express, in their own personal pledges, their commitment to things that are relevant to their own lives.
- **Taxonomic trick.** In teaching science, give students a known mnemonic such as **K**eep **P**lates **C**lean **O**r **F**amily **G**ets **S**ick to remember animal taxonomy: kingdom, phylum, class, order, family, genus, species.

Tell Me a Story

Overview

Tell Me a Story is the D-moment in which students are able to connect their experiences to the real world through storytelling. Throughout history, people have related their daily occurrences through word of mouth. In prehistoric civilizations, stories were told as a way to share important information, such as the location of food and shelter, and to warn of danger. The stories used exaggeration at times, as in a story of an enormous kill or a dangerous situation. In many cases, the stories were so elaborate that wonder, rather than fact, was being communicated. (Perhaps these were the first examples of "the one that got away" fish tales?) Stories were passed from one person to another, one village to another, one country to another. It gave the listening audience a chance to experience the event in their imaginations. Details and facts are important in depicting a life experience, but the telling can also be quite entertaining. This entertainment quality made the learning and sharing fun. In many cultures, storytelling has been raised to an art, not merely a way to record important events.

Today, storytelling is as valuable a communication tool as it ever was. Telling the story allows us to emphasize and highlight what we see as the important activities, facts, and events in our daily lives. Utilizing this modality in the classroom affords both the teacher and the student a chance to emphasize and elaborate on an essential issue, event, concept, or idea. This elaboration has a two-pronged outcome. Not only does it allow the storyteller to reinforce the concept through the story, but it also allows the audience to see the relationship of that story to the presenter. In effect, the storyteller reveals a good portion of his or her personal side as the events unfold.

Consequently, ***Tell Me a Story,*** with its millennia-old format, can teach, reinforce, and entertain. It will captivate students, challenge their thoughts, and engage their minds. It is a Quadrant D-moment at its best!

Pedagogy Perspective

Tell Me a Story is an ideal strategy for students with the following learning styles and intelligences.

Sensory Mode	Auditory
Thinking Modes	Concrete-Random Abstract-Random
Multiple Intelligences	Verbal/Linguistic Visual/Spatial Interpersonal

What Makes It High Rigor/Relevance?

This D-moment is high relevance because of the real-life connection. Students are relating their content knowledge of the curriculum, in either a real-life story or one of fantasy. Having the choice of fact or fiction allows students the opportunity to relay content knowledge in their own words and through their own lenses. This D-moment activity affords students the choice of using their imagination, in the case of fiction, or using their content vocabulary, in the case of fact, to relay a story.

Tell Me a Story also requires higher-level thinking skills, for students apply content known to them and weave it into fanciful stories. This helps them to remember or recall content knowledge or to explain concepts. Language is a shared system of sounds that represent objects and ideas that connect us to other humans. A quality education requires that we not only give children the ability to spell words correctly and create grammatically correct sentences with proper syntax, but that we also encourage them to communicate their rich experiences with words and gestures throughout the story. When we listen to the story, we not only listen to the words and ideas, but we also connect our emotions and recall past events. Storytelling uses the logical side of the brain's function to process the underlying structure of the story: sequence, plot line, and cause and effect. It also speaks to the conceptual side of the brain's function, which is to discern symbolic, intuitive, imaginative truth. Thus, storytelling helps the brain to integrate the message and its delivery into the whole, which promotes healthy development.

How to Use It

Tell Me a Story can be used at the beginning of the lesson, when introducing a new concept or attempting to capture students' attention. The story can be either a teaching strategy or a product of student work. Therefore, teachers can use the story to introduce the content to the students. The story may be told to engage the students with emotional hooks and vivid imagery, rather than lecturing or information recall. Next, the story can be a form of student work, in which students are asked to present the results of learning the concepts by telling a story or creative work of fiction that reemphasizes learned facts.

With this format, students will be more engaged in learning and will develop skills that will enhance not only vocabulary and communication but also, and ultimately, confidence and self-esteem. It is important to remember that storytelling must engage all students, either through listening or speaking. Following are several practices to create a classroom in which students learn storytelling skills.

- Tell a story to illustrate the important aspects of storytelling skills. This might begin with a personal story or one that students might know, such as a fable or folk tale. Students can model understanding by creating their own narrative.
- Display gestures, sounds, facial expressions, rhythm, timing, and any other visual presentation to elaborate on the physical part of the storytelling presentation. Do not be afraid to elaborate or exaggerate as you give this example.
- Brainstorm with students about how to write down their ideas for the storyline, emphasizing sequence of events and support-

ing facts, and jotting down details, descriptions, and keywords of information. Encourage flexibility in content and expression.

- Afford students the opportunity to speak comfortably in front of others.
- Incorporate group participation so that others might participate.
- Emphasize not only content skills, but linguistic skills as well.
- Build literacy skills through storytelling, emphasizing language, plot, syntax, and semantics.
- Practice telling the story with students in pairs. Keep changing partners, to build confidence in each student's ability to tell a story to small groups before giving the presentation to the entire class.
- Visualize the scenes.
- Answer the questions of *who, what, when, where, why*, and *how* to cover all the facts.
- Experiment with sounds and sound effects to add color to a presentation.
- Exaggerate words and phrases to emphasize a character or scene.
- Use body language and eye contact to emphasize ideas and captivate the audience.
- Try to use 3–5 senses in your stories. Describe how things look, feel, taste, smell, and sound by including colors, scents, and textures.

In some cases, students may be shy or apprehensive and have difficulty telling a story. Meeting with them individually, and encouraging them to think about the facts and the events and the people, will help. Let them know that every individual has the ability to be a storyteller and that their experiences are worth sharing.

Where to Use It

Following are some examples of using this D-moment in different subjects and at different grade levels.

All Grades

- **Figurative language.** After introducing proverbs, colloquialisms, or morals of fables in language arts, ask students to develop a story to relate an experience of their own that illustrates the phrase or concept behind each. For example, proverbs might include the following:
    - The pot calls the kettle black.
    - A watched pot never boils.
    - A stitch in time saves nine.
- **Historical script.** In social studies, have students retell a historic event from the perspective of a historic character. This character could emphasize a specific time in history and how he/she perceived it. The presentation could be simple or elaborate.
- **Storied concepts.** In studying social studies units on specific countries, or in science after finishing a unit, have students create and present a story using the components or concepts that they learned from the unit.
- **Trials and tribulations.** In science, have students take on the role of an important scientist or inventor and tell the story of the trials and tribulations of discovering or creating a new scientific phenomenon.

Grades Pre-K–5

- **Role playing.** Have students role-play "The Three Little Pigs" after listening to the story.
- **Fanciful words.** When teaching rhyming words and letters, have students take those words and create a fanciful story. Students will have to be able to spell the words in order to write them in their story. The story doesn't have to make sense; it could even be fanciful and funny. Encourage students to be creative and to enjoy not only the words, but the writing process as well.
- **A good thing?** After reading aloud the book *Chocolate Fever*, by Robert Kimmel Smith, have students create stories about having too much of a good thing.

- **Reporting the news.** Have students role-play being a television reporter. They report their views on "what's happening in the classroom." Students might take on different reporting personae, such as a local news, social studies, science, or math reporter.
- **Famous me.** Have students listen as you read aloud a story about a famous citizen. Then ask students to write a story that pertains to them as the main character, using the story facts.
- **Birthday story.** After reading a story aloud, have students create a story about the author's birthday. Students will tell the story of their own.
- **Vacation themes.** Just prior to a vacation break, have students create and present a story about what they plan to do over vacation. They must use vocabulary and themes that they have been studying. They may bring in props from home to add to their presentation.
- **Foreign adventure.** Read several different Magic Tree House books throughout the year. Have students write an adventure for Jack and Annie in a country from Asia, focusing on social studies standards for learning about other cultures.
- **Historical journal.** In history, have students use information that they learned in a lesson concerning a historical figure to write a daily journal entry as a person living in another time. Students may even dress up as they "become" that important figure.

Grades 6–12

- **Write your own ending.** Read a story. Review the main characters, theme, and plot line. Then have students create their own ending for the story as if they were the author.
- **Draw a cartoon.** Have students draw a cartoon, with captions, describing a concept recently presented. The cartoons should show that students have an understanding of the material. Ask each student to create a story around their cartoon.
- **Tell a tall tale.** When studying tall tales in language arts, have students research and learn elements of a tall tale. After reviewing examples of tall tales, have students create and present their own tall tales, including all the elements.

- **Reflect on appropriate behavior.** When teaching students about appropriate behaviors and expectations, have them create a story reflecting on expectations of appropriate behavior.
- **Graph the variables.** In math class, have students write stories to describe the situations being shown by line graphs. Students write two or three sentences to create a scenario that describes the rate of change and graph variables. Students then share their stories in class.
- **Illustrate physical laws.** In physics, have students take key laws of physics and create comic strips illustrating the concepts. Students then tell the story of their comic-strip creation.
- **Divide a cell.** When studying cell division in science class, group students together to tell a story of mitosis. Students draw a scale cutout of the chromosomes and create a story to describe what is happening in that specific phase.
- **Talk culture.** In social studies, after completing research on a specific culture, ask students to create a fact or fiction story. They must include several facts from within that specific lesson and create a storyline for the fictional part, including character, setting, problem, advance, solutions, and message. They may have prewriting conferences with groups of students to make sure that their stories make sense and that their facts are accurate. In the final presentation, students tell their stories.
- **Use words as a springboard.** When introducing new vocabulary words, have students create stories to give meaning to the words. Students then present a relevant story using the new vocabulary.
- **Write the rest.** When reading a book to a group, stop at the climax. Have students create the rest of the story and tell what they think is going to happen next. After writing down their conclusion, students tell their story as the author. When students finish, have them compare and contrast what others wrote. Then, finish the book as the author wrote it.
- **Become another life form.** In science, ask students to take a particular concept, such as the life cycle, and tell a story from the perspective of the plant, animal, or object being described in that particular lesson. (For example, you might have an animal talk

about its life experiences.) Have students work in pairs to create their stories and provide feedback.

- **Take yourself away.** Have students gather information about places, people, time periods, and events and then write a first-person story concerning the information they have gathered.
- **Tell a story in pictures.** Ask students to choose one element of literature studied recently in class. Have them make a five-slide digital story, using only pictures, to describe the element they chose. Students may use the Internet to search for the pictures or create the slides that will correspond to the element. Students also use a storyboard for elements for their ideas and pictures and then present that information orally in class.

What If?

Overview

What If? is a D-moment strategy that requires students to use their imagination and also think logically about the consequences of changing an event. ***What If?*** is similar to ***Future Think,*** in which students make predictions by thinking logically to predict some future event. ***What If?*** is more about examining current conditions and imagining impacts of change. For example, students might be asked to imagine what would be different today if specific historical events had not occurred or had occurred differently. By engaging in this thinking, students better recognize the impact of historical events. ***What If?*** can also be used to change the variables in a mathematical operation. For example, how would the slope of a line change if a variable in the equation being graphed were changed from a positive to a negative number? When students engage in this deeper thinking, they better understand slopes and graphing variables. In literature, ***What If?*** might explore how adding a new character would change the story. ***What If?*** is often used in science. For example, students might take an inquiry approach in discovering unifying concepts and underlying principles, as in the functions of human systems or cell reproduction.

What If? is a form of open-ended questioning. There rarely are single correct answers to these types of questions, and students are encouraged to think creatively and logically to arrive at their responses. Answers are usually detailed and thoughtful, and teachers listen for logical construction of an idea rather than specific content. ***What If?*** deepens students' understanding by requiring students to build upon the knowledge they have through looking at it from a different perspective.

Pedagogy Perspective

What If? is an ideal strategy for students with the following learning styles and intelligences.

Sensory Mode	Auditory
Thinking Modes	Abstract-Sequential Abstract-Random
Multiple Intelligences	Logical/Mathematical Existential

What Makes It High Rigor/Relevance?

Because of the open-ended nature of ***What If?*** questions, this D-moment strategy has the characteristics of high rigor. These questions drive thinking beyond the simple recall of an answer. When asked a ***What If?*** question, students will need to reflect on what knowledge they have of the subject and then connect that to other knowledge to create a logical hypothesis of what might believably happen as the result of a proposed change. This thinking process of posing, evaluating, selecting, and presenting a possible answer in response to a ***What If?*** question is very high rigor.

This D-moment also has high relevance, since the knowledge is often evaluated in the context of real-world implications and applications.

How to Use It?

Plan ahead with your questions. Few people can think of good, thoughtful, challenging questions on the spur of the moment. When teachers pose questions during a lesson, the natural tendency is to ask factual, low-level questions about the content. In order to have good, challenging ***What If?*** questions, think them through in advance and write them down. Have these as part of a lesson plan, so they can be appropriately selected and asked of students to challenge their thinking.

Be sure to give students sufficient time to respond to these questions. Many classrooms have a constant flow of conversations, and silence is often uncomfortable. But students need more time to think in order to properly answer a ***What If?*** question, as compared to a low-level question. Use extended wait time. Also, have students agree to the procedures you wish them to follow in answering, so they will know that this is a time for thoughtful, not quick, answers. Acknowledge that they often need to think and analyze before arriving at an answer. Use techniques that allow students to think quietly, to write, or to discuss with a table partner. All of these facilitation strategies are useful in slowing down the classroom activity and giving students better opportunity to think. The goal is to get students to think rigorously and not simply to cover "right" answers and then move on to the next topic.

One of the ways to make ***What If?*** questions even more relevant is to have students answer the question in a different role. Ask them to step out of the role of student and imagine themselves as a scientist, explorer, physician, or author. Then pose the ***What If?*** question to students and have them answer in that assigned role.

You can also use the ***What If?*** D–moment by encouraging students themselves to pose ***What If?*** questions. Students might pose these questions naturally. Be sure not to dismiss these questions when they occur. Perhaps the question can be redirected to the entire class to answer, or perhaps there's an opportunity to actually research the answer to a student's question. When students have the opportunity to research the answer to a question, they are more likely to retain the information that they discover. Encourage students to ask ***What If?*** questions; perhaps even give an assignment in which students are expected to pose a number of ***What If?*** questions.

In facilitating the discussion, teachers need to be knowledgeable on the topic and willing to enter unfamiliar territory. Teachers need to be ready to accept students' responses with some degree of plausibility and to make connections between students' questions and the topic they are expected to learn, related to standards.

Where to Use It?

Following are some examples of using this D-moment in different subjects and at different grade levels.

All Grades

- **Writing prompts.** ***What If?*** questions are excellent prompts for student writing assignments.
- **Student-posed questions.** After studying a unit, have students create their own ***What If?*** questions and pose these for other groups of students to answer.
- **Oral stories.** Rather than asking students to write immediately, have them create oral stories in answer to a ***What If?*** question. Perhaps have students write and elaborate. Students may be more creative and let ideas flow more in storytelling than in writing.

Grades Pre-K–5

- **Pet predictions.** Ask students who have pets to identify the kinds of animals they have as pets. Have students make a list of the tasks involved in taking care of pets and then make predictions about what would happen if they didn't take care of their pet.
- **No more cars.** Have students illustrate and write about what their lives would be like if all cars stopped working.
- **New character in town.** In reading class, after students have read a story, ask them to take the main character from the story and place him/her in their city as the setting. Have students elaborate on how the story would be different.
- **Music piracy.** When discussing copyright laws and piracy, pose a scenario in which everyone could copy and share music freely. What do students think would be different in our world?
- **Clothing forecast.** Have pre-K students look at the weather forecast and discuss appropriate and inappropriate clothing to wear the next day.

- **Earth spin.** When introducing Earth science, pose questions to students such as "What if the Earth stopped spinning?" or "What if the Earth changed the speed it was spinning each day?" or "What if the Earth started spinning faster?" Have students write about what would be different in our world.
- **Data switch.** Have students look at a graph of data that reports averages. Ask students how it would look if the data showed the median or mode instead.

Grades 6–12

- **Secret ingredients.** When studying nutrition and reading nutritional labels, have students make predictions as to what would happen to the quality of the product, taste of the product, or shelf life if the ingredients in the product were changed.
- **New identity.** In English language arts, as students are reading a historical narrative, take time for students to imagine themselves as a character in the story and see if they would follow the same actions as the character. For example, in reading *The Canterbury Tales,* ask students to relate where they would go on their own pilgrimage.
- **The way it wasn't.** In history, have students predict what would be different today if specific historical events had turned out differently (for example, if the South had successfully seceded from the United States or the United States had not acquired the lands of the Louisiana Purchase).
- **Different endings.** When studying English historical figures, have students consider how events might have turned out differently. For example, Mary I, Queen of England, married Philip II of Spain and wanted a child to seal the two countries together, making England a stronger Catholic country. They never had a child, and the throne passed to Elizabeth I; the country became Protestant again. Pose these questions: "What if Mary and Philip had had a son?" "What language would we speak?" "Would we have a national religion?" "Would the Pilgrims have ever come here?"

"Why" Questions

Overview

We are all familiar with the famous six question stems: *who, what, when, where, why,* and *how*. Each of these questions seeks to uncover knowledge. Yet, the most powerful of these is the question that starts with *why*. The other five often are convergent questions; they focus on a specific answer, and there are usually a limited number of answers or a single answer. The *why* question is more divergent; the answer is likely to draw in more related knowledge, and it often generates more *why* questions.

Young children often frustrate their parents with repetitious *why* questions. Think about the difference between the questions "When was I born?" versus "Why was I born?" or the difference between "What is the color of an apple?" and "Why is the apple red?" There is usually no simple answer to a *why* question. If a parent gives an answer, it usually does not satisfy the child and frequently leads to more questions. "Why" questions are powerful learning questions.

Scientists probe for new discoveries, simply following *why* questions and seeking to examine underlying principles of the world in which we live. Technicians seeking to correct an engineering problem start with the question "Why did this fail?" Uncovering answers to that technical question leads to innovation and improvement.

In the classroom, expose students to *why* questions and challenge them to uncover greater knowledge. Also, seek to have students develop the practice of using *why* questions to direct their own learning. ***"Why" Questions*** as a D-moment is about the more frequent use of the question *why* by both teacher and students.

Pedagogy Perspective

"Why" Questions is an ideal strategy for students with the following learning styles and intelligences.

Sensory Mode	Auditory
Thinking Modes	Concrete-Sequential Abstract-Sequential
Multiple Intelligences	Verbal/Linguistic Logical/Mathematical Existential

What Makes It High Rigor/Relevance?

Whether students are asked a *why* question or posing one themselves, there is higher-level thinking involved. *Why* questions are not short answer. To answer a *why* question requires linking several bits of prior knowledge into a logical answer. The question may be so challenging that research is necessary before a student can answer. In all cases, to answer this type of question effectively, students have to think at higher levels — what is referred to as rigorous thinking. The act of posing questions is an example of rigor as well. Students must have a breadth of knowledge to be able to pose a question. In addition, the *why* question demonstrates interest and a desire to learn more and seek further explanation. This is where the relevance occurs. When students are able to pose *why* questions about a subject, they see the importance of the topic being explored, have a desire to learn more, and see the application to their world. When students are posing and (hopefully) answering their own *why* questions, they are more likely prepared for the challenges of the real world at a level of high rigor and high relevance.

How to Use It

Beyond basic literacy and mathematical reasoning, one of the greatest skills that enables students to be lifelong learners is the ability to pose their own questions.

One of the challenges for teachers, when asking students to generate their own questions, is that teachers need to be prepared to hear questions that they may not be able to answer. If teachers take the role of the "all-knowing source of knowledge" in the classroom, these difficult questions may shatter that image. Teachers need to be comfortable in confronting student questions that go beyond their existing knowledge.

Imagine that students in history class have been taught only answers — perhaps several thousand historical facts. These students might be incapable of generating interesting hypotheses, inferences, or questions about history. They would see history as little more than a set of facts, where everything is decided and little can be changed. Learning answers without learning questions produces a kind of ideology in which everything is already settled. Teachers must empower students to believe that they can change the course of human events in the future by posing questions and not accepting current affairs as "that is just the way it is."

Following are several practices to create a classroom in which students begin to ask more *why* questions.

- **Provide modeling.** We all learn from seeing others model certain behaviors. One of the ways for students to acquire the skill of posing good *why* questions is observing the teacher doing exactly that. Constantly pose *why* questions on the curriculum, and focus student attention to the examples of those questions that seek further knowledge and understanding.
- **Acknowledge that not every question has an answer.** Acknowledge that some questions remain unanswered, for our world and human behavior still have complexities for which we do not know the answer. Be open and honest with students in this. Realize that sometimes just asking the question leads to a higher level of thinking and understanding.

- **Be open to new possibilities.** For students to ask a *why* question, they must recognize that there are multiple possibilities or perspectives to an observation. Any event or object can be observed from various perspectives, and there are always new possibilities. For example, eating a simple meal seems to be a necessary physiological function. But to go further, we can look at healthy preparation methods, nutritional aspects, cultural aspects of food, environmental contaminants, economic implications, and even the moral perspective when we reflect on those who live with hunger. When students realize that multiple possibilities exist, it is easier to begin to pose questions.
- **Differentiate opinion and perspective.** Frequently, differences are attributed to opinions. When two people see the same thing, yet respond differently, we call that a difference of opinion. For example, a vegetarian and a carnivore have "differing opinions" about prepared steak. We attribute the differences to a difference in opinion when the person matches the observation with their values. Yet they have the same perspective, because they "see" the same steak. An illustration of different perspectives might occur when a meat inspector and a chef look at a steak: One is looking for cleanliness, and the other is looking for tastiness. These are differences in perspective. If we attribute differences only to opinion, we close off our thinking that differences are caused only by differences in values, and we blind ourselves to looking at things differently.
- **Nurture the classroom.** The classroom environment makes a difference in whether students feel comfortable in asking questions. The classroom must be free, but not too free; safe, but not too safe. The tone may be playful and creative, but the classroom needs enough regularity that chaos is controlled, allowing students to think, converse, listen, and question without feeling either made fun of or lost.
- **Be comfortable with silence.** In the rush of teaching, we fill every second with conversation and activity to keep students occupied. High-level thinking and posing questions requires some time. Use wait time when posing questions or asking students to create questions. Students and teachers need to be comfortable with silence for taking time to think and reflect.

Where to Use It

Following are some examples of using this D-moment in different subjects and at different grade levels.

All Grades

- **Science or history.** After a lesson in which students are introduced to new information, have the students write on the top half of the card something they have learned. On the bottom half of the card, students write a new question related to what more they want to learn. Go around the room and have all students share their new questions.

Grades Pre-K–5

- **Book titles.** After reading aloud *White Socks Only*, by Evelyn Coleman, have students pose questions about why the author selected *White Socks Only* as the title. Have students create another title for the story.
- **Pause for complex reading.** When reading a text aloud, stop at intervals for students to think about parts of the text that are confusing or about which they have questions. Students mark the points of text that seem confusing or about which they have questions. Have students reread those sections and ask questions.
- **Science observations.** Set up a fish tank and plants in the classroom. There are many animal species that could be used in this activity. Have students make observations about the growing fish, animals, or plants and then research the answers to their *why* questions.
- **Science inquiry.** Have students pose *why* questions in science. After reading the nonfiction book *Ants*, by Melissa Stewart, focus on the part where the ants form a bridge so that the rest of the ants can cross a body of water. What happened to the ants that formed the bridge? Why did they do that? This could be a typical question on students' minds.
- **Current events.** Choose a controversial issue being debated in current events. Before having students begin to take sides, dis-

cuss the issue. Have small groups of students just create questions that start with *why*. These might include "Why is this important?", "Why is this so controversial?", and "Why does this affect me?"

- **Endangered species.** As 1st-grade students are beginning to study and research animal species, have them come up with *why* questions related to endangered species. Have students discuss what can be done to help protect the animals. This could be extended in group research projects.
- **Metric system.** When studying the metric system, ask students, "Why does the United States use the English measurement system rather than the metric system?" and "What barriers would the United States encounter if it tried to force the metric system on everyone?"
- **Natural disasters.** Show students an unusual photo of an event such as an earthquake, volcanic eruption, or hurricane. Ask students to pose questions that relate to what they see in the picture.
- **Forms of government.** When introducing the basic forms of government, have students pose questions about why different forms of government have different characteristics. Then give students time to research and come back and answer as many of the questions as possible.
- **Physical education.** Have students make connections between playing as a team and working in the real world.

Grades 6–12

- **Reading.** While reading *Of Mice and Men*, form students into groups to develop one or two *why* questions (for example, "Why does George choose to shoot and kill Lennie?") and write those questions on a large sheet of plain paper. Engage students in the silent conversation, having them individually respond to the *why* questions on the large white paper. There is no talking, and they communicate only on the paper. Students can respond to questions or add to comments that other students have made.
- **History.** When studying Egypt and mummification, show a clip from a movie in which mummies chase after the characters. Ask

students whether mummies can come to life; then have students conduct research to answer the question. Students can also do a compare-and-contrast about mummies in history versus those in movies.

- **English warm-up.** As students walk into the classroom, have them immediately pick up a warm-up paper that has a *why* question. (Examples include "Why read?" and "Why do we have schools?") Students quietly answer the *why* question individually. Have students share individual entries with two or three others and then share group answers with the class.
- **Library.** In the library, have students create a list of questions that they would ask their favorite author if they were to meet. Students then research to try to find answers to their questions and create an interview dialogue as the final performance task.
- **Grammar.** Give students a sentence and explain why the structure is correct. Then provide a different but parallel example of the same sentence. Have students substitute nouns and verbs within the sentence to change the meaning but retain the structure.
- **English.** When beginning a story, have students make predictions based upon just the title/cover illustration. As the story is read, ask why they made their predictions. Stop and ask students what they think about the specific situation and scenario (for example, "Why did this happen?" or "Have you ever experienced something similar?"). Give students plenty of time to think, and allow them to pass and work on an additional answer if they cannot think of an immediate response.